New Horizon in Male-Female Relationships

New Horizon in Male-Female Relationships

David Samuel Green

with Sandra Eleanor McDermott
Foreword by Barrington Davidson

RESOURCE *Publications* • Eugene, Oregon

NEW HORIZON IN MALE-FEMALE RELATIONSHIPS

Copyright © 2010 David Samuel Green. All rights reserved. Except for brief quotations in critical publications or reviews, no part of this book may be reproduced in any manner without prior written permission from the publisher. Write: Permissions, Wipf and Stock Publishers, 199 W. 8th Ave., Suite 3, Eugene, OR 97401.

Resource Publications
An Imprint of Wipf and Stock Publishers
199 W. 8th Ave., Suite 3
Eugene, OR 97401
www.wipfandstock.com

ISBN 13: 978-1-60899-428-1

Manufactured in the U.S.A.

To Amoy Marshall Green
My wonderful wife
You have empowered me to think
at a different level in our marriage of almost a decade.

> "The significant problems we face cannot be solved at the same level of thinking we were at when we created them."
>
> ALBERT EINSTEIN (1879 TO 1955)

Contents

List of Figures ix
Foreword by Barrington Davidson xi
Preface by Sandra Eleanor McDermott xiii
Author's Preface xvii
Acknowledgments xix

1. Introduction 1
2. Sociological and Theological Anthropology on Marriage and Equality 5
3. The Historicity of Marriage 11
4. Common Problems and Reasons for Marital Failure 28
5. Conceptualizing Love 37
6. The Historicity of Human Sexuality 54
7. Conceptualizing Marriage 63
8. Applying the Golden Rule and Developing Marital Automaticity 73
9. The Master Plan of Marriage and the Marital Love Cycle 77
10. Servanthood in Male-Female Relationship 85
11. Applying the Concepts of Product Thinking, Egalitarianism and Authentic Love 99
12. Marshalling Marital Skills 116
13. Conclusion 136

Glossary 141
Bibliography 147
Subject/Name Index 155

List of Figures

1. The Johari Window of Love 47
2. Number of times per year that men in the United Sates have intercourse 60
3. Marital Love Cycle 79
4. Service Quadrants 88
5. Cycle of Love Making 93
6. The Four Marital Seasons 105
7. A Basic Model of the Communication Process 118
8. Process of Marital Communication 120
9. Development of Conflict 124
10. Management of Self in Relations to Conflict 125
11. Effects of Attitude 126
12. Authentic Love 128

Foreword

IN THIS NEW BOOK, *New Horizon in Male-Female Relationships*, David Samuel Green is advocating that men and women set about deliberately transforming their cognitive constructs from those based on the old patriarchal influences to new ones, based on egalitarianism, having regard to changed socio-economic realities. For example, the fact that women now share equally in "bringing home the bacon."

He posits that changes in socio-economic realities demand a change in cognitions, a new mindset as regards male-female relationships. He is saying it cannot be business as usual in marital relationships, that changes must be made taking account of new male-female alignments and roles.

Green introduces the idea of "product thinking" an interesting concept that will be of special interest to the mathematicians among the readership. This brings to the table a fresh perspective, which he is saying, if applied, will revitalise family life and, in particular, marriage relationships.

In this well-researched volume, Green has managed to give the reader the benefit of his own conceptualization of marriage or provide a comprehensive review of existing literature dealing with a range of marital issues. He also outlines practical steps which may be taken toward achieving more satisfying family relationships.

Some readers while giving credence to the product thinking perspective being advocated by Green, may dismiss the practice of it, outlined in the later chapters, as being idealistic. However, this new perspective deserves consideration. It should be put in the mix as another approach to handle male - female relationships that will work for many persons and together with all the other approaches, help to impact our family interactions for the better as well as improve family interactions for generations to come. I congratulate David Samuel Green for launching out into new frontiers of thought.

Dr. Barrington Davidson
CEO, Family Life Ministries
Kingston, Jamaica

Preface

MARRIAGE AS A SOCIAL institution has been an indelible part of the cultural landscape of humanity for centuries. Considered to be one of the main philosophical pillars on which human civilization is predicated, marriage can be construed as a societal arrangement that is enshrouded by a legal contract between individuals with the purpose of the continual propagation of the human specie.

The impact of the marital relationship as an entrenched socio-cultural institution steeped in deep historical patriarchal origins cannot be overstated. The production of the Engelian nineteenth century scholarly treatise on *The Origins of the Family, Private Property and the State* provided the backdrop for a progressive dialectic in reaction to a longstanding détente of historical proportions between two colossal political systems. The nineteenth century proved to be pivotal in stirring the cauldron of opposing political philosophical thought with the indomitable rise of Capitalism on a collision course with the appealing popularity of Marxian Socialism. The Industrial Revolution as a seminal event witnessed the spiraling rise of two powerful political forces reacting to the rise of Industrial Revolution and the attendant issues in relation to private property, class, and male dominance in relation to female subjugation.

Frederick Engels' seminal work portends a comprehensive historical review of the meteoric rise of the Consanguine Family within patriarchal strands. Engels' interpretation of the economic conditions emanating from the Industrial Revolution had certainly set the wheels in motion for the continuity of the scholarly debate of Conservative Idealism versus Liberal Feminist thought coexisting in ideological détente. For example, in analyzing the nature of the marriage bond on the impact of the family within the organized strata of society, Conservatism as a soaring political rhetoric championed the family as indispensable to industrialized civilization in the form of a long term commitment to emotional stability and the bastion of cultural values. Thus, for the Conservative argument, the absence of the family signaled the imminent destruction of a predetermined cultural ethos which would have been a catalyst for social anarchy of societal and moral value systems.

On the other side of the political spectrum, the twentieth century marked the rise of the Women's Movement out of which Gender Feminism as a radical ideology became the tour de force of opposition to the Conservative ideal in the unleashing of an incessant diatribe against social institutions of marriage and the family. Radicalized Feminism's revolt was against the perceived linkages of women's economic and political entrapment to familial domestication and the tyranny of Capitalism. The latter's political argument was to place a premium on the family as a bastion of traditional social, moral and cultural values.

Radicalized elements within the Women's Movement have argued that the nexus of family systems to Patriarchal Capitalism was considered formidable source of women's oppression. For example, Gender Feminists look at the role of the patriarchal family in the *Diary of a Mad Housewife*, which was a 1960s novel written by author Sue Kaufman, who chronicled the angst of an upper middle class urban housewife. Kaufman further opined that some of the evils stemming from a patriarchal marital bond were domestic violence, which in that era was considered to be unfiltered expressions of the married state. Gender Feminism equated marriage as an involuntary state and tantamount to slavery as the prevailing thinking was to view the social role of women as chattel. Gender Feminism also was impacted by Marxian dogma in its animus against the negating influence of Capitalism. The Marxian dogma alluded to the functions of marriage and the family as integrative components within the Capitalist stock including private property, class structure, and the mode and factors of economic production.

No doubt, the ongoing philosophical debates on the marriage-family debacle witnessed the rise of the nascent Liberal Feminism within the ranks of the Women's Movement. Liberal Feminism rise to prominence not only exposed gaping fissures of opposing viewpoints but sought to muzzle the voice of the Gender Feminists and to temper the flames of the anti marriage rhetoric with reference to Betty Friedan's pivotal work, *The Feminine Mystique* (1963).

In this important historical work, Friedan represented the thrust of the progressive Feminist philosophical movement by advancing the argument that women of the 1960s were enslaved by domesticity and defined by their roles as mother and wife. Although she called the family a "comfortable concentration camp," it is noteworthy to note that Friedan's goal was not to eliminate marriage but to ensure that the marital bonds represented a sense of equity of the division of labor in a capitalist society (Friedan, 1963). In interpreting Friedan's work, it appeared that the goals of egalitarianism were the thrust of her argument and suggested that women had the inalienable right to achieve happiness, maximize their potential, and lead productive lives outside of the marital relationship.

Having made an investigation into the ideals of Liberal Feminist thought, the book *New Horizon in Male-Female Relationships* attempts to bridge the philosophical divide between the idealism of Liberal Feminism and hard line core values of Gender Feminism. The work reflects a synthesis of adapting salient principles of Engelian dogma as in the comprehensive treatment of the historicity of marriage and the importance of the core values of Liberal Feminism regarding the place of Marriage and family in cultural and geopolitical societies.

The book is timely in that it offers the lay reader a panoramic picture of the historical events surrounding the nineteenth and twentieth centuries, which paved the way for the primarily philosophical posturing of those eras:- "There was a women's movement that criticized war as male ejaculation. It criticized marriage and the family as institutional crucibles of male privilege. . . . Some criticized sex, including the institution of intercourse, as a strategy and practice in subordination" (Mackinnon, 1987, 1989).

New Horizon in Male-Female Relationships should be viewed as a titillating and yet reactionary scholarly genre. A genre which would not only add quality and depth to the Marriage and Family literature, but there is an attempt to sooth the bruising psychological wounds sustained from centuries of heated debate over the role of Marriage and Family in contemporary society. The panacea offered would stem the rising tide of divorce and marital tension, which was highlighted as having roots in the bedrock of patriarchal power structure and principles.

The advancement of Product Thinking as a new thrust conceptualized marriage as a unitary principle, which is predicated on the process of proactive thinking. Product Thinking forms an intricate dialectic in examining the marital and family bonds from the discipline of sociology, anthropology and theology. The scholarly piece attempts to contextualize the idealized notion of the marital relationship through an extraordinary appeal to the Judeo-Christian religious narrative, which also has indelible roots in patriarchy.

The main thrust of the book is to provide a historical foray into the rationale for marital failures and underscore how Product Thinking as a revolutionary concept will foster the egalitarian ideal in changing the mindset of the patriarchal past. The book provides the basis for further discussion or investigation of male-female relationships representative by the following philosophical and socio-cultural tenets: (1) the Sociocultural approach, which examines the reasons for the forces of violence and aggression against women that are tolerated as normative by society; (2) the Psychological approach, which examines the emotional reasons for men being abusive and dominant in the marital relationship and why women accept it; and (3) the Class analysis approach, which is a tenet of patriarchal capitalism that reinforces the notion of male dominance in the attempt to retain their place in the patriarchal power structure.

Although written primarily for an academic audience, the book does offer universal appeal to a wider swath of non-academicians. *New Horizon in Male-Female Relationships* invites the reader to a motivational journey of scholarly analysis in understanding the pivotal period, which undergirded the historical tensions underlying the Marriage and Family debacle. The appeal from Judeo-Christian philosophical thought attempts to reinvent the wheel of a parallel alternative of servanthood. This would be viewed as revolutionary interpretation and departure from contemporary theological thought in relation to Biblical Scriptures. The concept of Servant is conceptualized in a theological context that would advance the marital relationship as an egalitarian ideal in place of a hierarchical marital relationship as a proffered solution to this irritating conundrum.

Dr. Sandra Eleanor McDermott, Psy.D., LLP, CCFC
February 10, 2010
Kingston, Jamaica

Author's Preface

THIS GENERATION IS FACED with divorce at an unprecedented rate as a result of economic, social, and theological shifts. A system of marriage and social policies, based on patriarchy as a cultural system, has proven to be both deficient and bankrupt in this postmodern era of female liberation and equal opportunity. The liberation of women brings with it concomitant challenges such as the striving for independence and individuality in marriage by both sexes, given the pervasiveness of individualism in especially Western societies. An individualistic attitude in marriage continues to pose a serious challenge to the longevity of the relationship due to the stronghold of our patriarchal legacy. A new paradigm to advance the merit of "product thinking" is therefore warranted to mitigate the phenomenal divorce rate in this and successive generations to come. Research affirms that divorce tends to run in families. The author proposes a new mindset in the form of "product thinking," in tandem with the rediscovery and application of compassion or forgiveness to support the egalitarian philosophy of marriage. Product thinking is essential to ensure marital satisfaction and stability for future generations.

The author also examines the sociology of marriage and theological treaties on discussions of marriage and equality, which forms the foundation for a new paradigm in marital relation. The literature review and biblical texts from a Christian perspective chronicle the historicity of marriage from both evolutionary and Judeo-Christian perspectives to explain the concept and demonstrate that the genesis of marriage is based on patriarchy, which is rooted in injustice toward the sexes. The marriage literature was replete in reference to common problems and the reasons for marital failures. There needs to be a new conceptualization of love with compassion as an important element to create a roborant for marriage. The understanding of human sexuality is based on historicity, which the author illustrates through the practical application of "product thinking" as a revolutionary concept in marital relationships. Product thinking will enhance intimacy with compassion or forgiveness, and egalitarianism in the male-female relationships.

The book is primarily aimed at the academics who share the need to preserve scholarship. However, the book does provide information which would be suitable for non-academic readers, including counselors, students, theologians, pastors and other professionals who will find it of significant value. Given our changing context, we have to think at a higher cognitive level than we have in the past because the problems we face cannot be solved at the same level of thinking that originally created them. The book also caters to both undergraduate and graduate students in a variety of academic disciplines, including psychology, counseling, marriage and family therapy, family life education, pastoral counseling, and sociology.

The book's contribution to current scholarship lies in its extensive treatment of marriage from both evolutionary and Judeo-Christian perspectives. Furthermore, it provides a history of patriarchy and its impact on male-female relationships, with the author advancing potent argument to enhance the concept of egalitarianism while presenting product thinking as a new paradigm for understanding the marital union. The themes analyzed reinforce the need for a new paradigm and the concepts explored are plausible for the cognitive restructuring and resocialization that are necessary for the creation of harmony between the sexes in all spheres of life and human endeavors.

David Samuel Green
November 20, 2009
Montego Bay, Jamaica

Acknowledgments

MAKING A SIGNIFICANT CONTRIBUTION to scholarship can be painstaking as the process demands commitment, critical thinking, courage, and collaboration. It feeds on the cheer and consolation offered by some peers and the criticism leveled by others. Therefore, it is imperative to express gratitude to those who played a part in the completion of this project, as well as those who stimulated clarity of thought and expression through their caustic remarks.

Special thanks to Dr. Jennifer Cooper, Stephanie Ambersley, Lenworth and Hyacinth Anglin, Dr. Yves Bergeron, Dr. Kent Maxwell and Dr. Dave Gosse for their feedback on a previous manuscript in which some of the major concepts in this book were seeded. Heartfelt thanks to Dr. Sandra McDermott for reviewing an initial draft of this book and serving as developmental editor, spending many hours in editing and consultation. Thanks to Dr. Barrington Davidson and his assistant Kathy Roberts for their review of the manuscript and Dr. Davidson's kindness in offering a foreword. Finally, to my wife Amoy, for her cheer and understanding when I had to spend hours in concentrated research or left home at short notice to travel miles away for consultations.

1

Introduction

As the world advances in science and technology, we are faced with unprecedented changes and challenges. Covey (2004) sums up our current state well in his conclusion that "the challenges and complexities we face in our personal lives and relationships, in our families . . . are of a different order of magnitude" (p. 3). History revealed that progress necessitates concomitant changes and challenges. For centuries, the changes and challenges were met with relevant questions that resulted in answers that shaped direction in each generation because new discoveries inevitably affect thought and culture.

The family and marriage have evolved through the centuries. At the same time, thought and culture have facilitated female inferiority and male dominance. The repression of women through lack of equal opportunity resulted in a cultural imbalance as women became faithful to the institution of marriage out of necessity. However, new socio-cultural trends have resulted in an emerging astronomical divorce rate, which has forced a rethinking of our understanding of marriage and family. The problems marriages face in this era are directly related to our way of thinking. In order to deal effectively with these problems we have to think and act differently. Einstein is noted for his conclusion that "the significant problems we face cannot be solved at the same level of thinking we were at when we created them" (Covey, 2004, p. 19).

Life is filled with both tight spots and nice spots. The inherent difficulties in handling the challenges of the "tight spots" and preventing the "nice spots" from becoming tight spots suggest a continuous struggle to find meaning and significance in every area of life. One of the most complex areas of life is the marital relationship. Due to the intimate nature of marriage, there is a great possibility for both banes and boons to arise as one seeks to navigate both the tight spots and nice spots.

This generation is experiencing divorce and remarriage at an unprecedented rate. Nevertheless, researchers affirm that although marital problems will be experienced during the marital journey, marital success is highly possible even for troubled marriages. A marriage does not have to be a trial and error experiment, as one does not have to resort to unmarried cohabitation in the form of trial marriage or as an alternative to marriage, given the history of the marriage phenomenon, which has recipes for both failure and success. It is possible to learn from what research literature has revealed regarding the past experiences of others in order to achieve marital success.

Worthington (1990) conceptualized a psychology of marriage as "placing two gear wheels close to each other" (p. 30). He stated that what actually happens when they come together depends on four things: 1) the communication that takes place between them; 2) the closeness of the gears; 3) the conflict that develops; 4) the contact that is maintained between them through the conflict (p. 30). Worthington (1990) built his psychology of marriage on the concepts of communication, closeness, conflict, commitment, change and stability. Although these are some key building blocks, this viewpoint fails to address some key components, such as mental processes, behaviors, emotions and socio-cultural and economic impact.

The patriarchal approach to marriage seen in traditional marriages has inhibited marital happiness in many respects by perpetuating inequality. For example, women are treated as inferior to men and the inequality of the gender role has failed to foster the mental and practical attitudes needed for empowerment in marriage. Therefore, an egalitarian approach to marriage seems a more attractive alternative in order to facilitate marital success through mutual empowerment and to maximize each spouse's potential due to the new trends in modern romantic relationships.

Researchers have confirmed that several things which would be tolerated in ordinary relationships may "become intolerable in the intimate relationship of sexual union" (Ellis, 1910, p. 448). Initial love and continuation of love are important for marital satisfaction (Weisfeld, 1997). Divorce is on the increase and young people have been asking crucial questions about marriage for decades (Carter and Foley, 1943). While monogamy is the best foundation for marital satisfaction, egalitarianism is equally important for marital satisfaction (Weisfeld, 1997). The church in the Western hemisphere has changed her theology about women in ministry due to socio-cultural trends. Women have increased economic independence and mobility, which are shattering cultural stereotypes and revolutionizing marriage (Dunlap, 1935). These changes support the need for a new paradigm both at the cognitive and behavioral levels, if marriages are to be successful and fulfilling.

However, the mindset of couples has not changed to accommodate the new trends. Women are becoming more independent due to career advancement and changing social roles, which have empowered women to participate equally in providing for the family and to decide whom and when to marry. Hansen et al. (1994) observe that "the problems inherent in dual-career marriages are significant, and couples frequently need assistance in working through potential and real concerns" (p. 347). Many of these concerns, such as sex-roles, decision making, household and childrearing responsibilities, revolve around the negative effects of a patriarchal approach to the marital relationship. This implies that an egalitarian mindset is indispensable to a successful marriage, consistent with the cognitive behavioral perspective that thoughts affect feelings and actions either consciously or unconsciously (Dobson, 2001).

The criteria for a healthy marriage discussed in the literature suggest that an egalitarian marriage is the best way to meet the requirements of a mutually satisfying relationship. Egalitarianism requires the understanding of marriage as a single entity. It is more than a relationship (Lozoff, as cited in Swift, 1998), based on the following: commitment (Adams and Jones, 1997); sharing of household and childrearing responsibilities (Schwartz, 1998); avoidance of power struggle on the basis of money (Blumstein & Schwartz as cited in Dakins & Wampler, 2008); forgiveness or willingness to change or accept responsibility for change and love (Whisman, et al., 1997).

There is the need for a paradigm shift in how we understand male-female relationships. Western current thought and culture survival elevate the ethos of independence that undermines the necessity for interdependence. This new paradigm therefore requires thinking at a different level than we thought in the past. This kind of thinking makes love a verb, so that in improving one's marital situation, one works on the one thing that he or she has control over—him or herself (Covey, 1989, 2004). The product thinking paradigm (a new way of conceptualizing marriage as a union) as the new way of thinking and being is built on principles that allow a marriage partner to be positively proactive in building a successful marital relationship despite the challenges. Product thinking has the potency to stimulate key mental processes and behaviors that are essential for marital success in this period of history and future generations. Product thinking, guided by an egalitarian approach with mutual influence, seems to be the best way forward. This recommendation is guided by the notion that product thinking engenders cognitive change and stimulates egalitarianism at the behavioral level.

The ways in which the concepts of marital union, love, and forgiveness or compassion are conceptualized will have a significant negative or positive impact on one's marriage. Therefore, a proper understanding of love, the marital union and forgiveness or compassion, as well as familiarity with important research findings on human sexuality, intimacy and other areas of marriage, is integral to a successful marriage.

The main thesis of this book is that an egalitarian marriage should be guided by product thinking, compassion, awareness and practice as factors that foster a successful marriage in this period of human history and in the future. Arguments for this kind of relationship will be established on an analysis of the history of marriage, a review of the literature on common marital problems, an examination of the predictors of marital success, a new paradigm for conceptualizing marriage and love, the basis for an egalitarian marriage, and the marital skills necessary for a successful marriage. Special attention will also be given to the history of human sexuality and its implications for sexual adjustment and satisfaction.

It will be demonstrated that marriage has had a patriarchal legacy that has done injustice to the sexes, especially to women. Patriarchy continues to negatively influence the behavior of men and women both at the conscious and unconscious levels. The instrumental leadership role (the administrative functions that ensure behaviors allow for the achievement of goals) and expressive leadership role (resolving the tensions that are caused by behavioral demands), which are fundamental to marital success, are best fulfilled in an egalitarian relationship in this era as well as in the future. The true egalitarian ideal is built on product thinking, authentic love, and a proper understanding of human sexuality.

2

Sociological and Theological Anthropology on Marriage and Equality

DIFFICULTIES INHERENT IN TRYING to reconstruct the family from the earliest possible stage are summed up appropriately in the introduction of Westermarck (1901). The writer observes that:

> The origin and development of human marriage have been discussed by such eminent writers as Darwin, Spencer, Morgan, Lubbock, and many others. On some of the more important questions involved in it all these writers are in general accord, and this agreement has led to their opinions being widely accepted as if they were well-established conclusions of science. But on several of these points Mr. Westermarck has arrived at different, and sometimes diametrically opposite, conclusions, and he has done so after a most complete and painstaking investigation of all the available facts. (Westermarck, 1901, p. v)

The following is a telling commentary on the divergent views on this important subject. One's presuppositions will affect his or her analysis and determine the conclusion that is reached on the phenomenon. Engels (1972) disagrees with Westermarck (1901) by stating that there was primitive promiscuity. Engels (1972) asserts that:

> Before the beginning of the sixties, one cannot speak of a history of the family. In this field, the science of history was still completely under the influence of the Five Books of Moses. The patriarchal form of the family, which was there described in greater detail than anywhere else, was not only assumed without question to be the oldest form, but it was also identified—minus its polygamy—with the bourgeois family of today, as if the family had really experienced no historical development at all. (p. 74–75)

Engels (1972) discounts the veracity of biblical history in favor of an evolutionary perspective. However, his declaration underpins the tension that exists between the theological presuppositions and the evolutionary presuppositions on the subject.

From an evolutionary perspective, "the study of the history of the family dates from 1861, from the publication of Bachofen's Mutterrecht" (Engels 1972, p. 75). Bachofen (as cited in Engels, 1972) argues for primitive promiscuity resulting in uncertain paternity of offspring, causing lineage to be traceable only in the female line in antiquity without exception. This issue of female lineage gave women a place of honor and resulted in matriarchy or gynaecocracy. There was finally a transition to monogamy involving the violation of primitive religious rule. The claims have been advanced supposedly with evidence from ancient classic literature.

McLennan (as cited in Engels, 1972) was the second person to examine the history of the family. He did not know about Bachofen and he came to opposite conclusions. In his view, the first people were exogamous and the second endogamous. His theory was not well established, and he was thus generally referred to as the founder of the history of human family and leading scholar in the discipline. "McLennan knew only three forms of marriage: polygyny, polyandry and monogamy" (Engels, 1972, p. 80). It is argued that he overlooked the evidence suggesting communal marriage or primitive promiscuity, which Lubbock (in The origin of Civilization, 1870) used evidence to support as an historical reality (Engels, 1972). Morgan (as cited in Engels, 1972) is credited for organizing human history into the categories of savagery, barbarism and civilization. He also argued for primitive promiscuity.

The lower stage of savagery in Morgan's proposal is based on deductive reasoning on the basis of an evolutionary theory because no direct evidence is available to prove its existence. As a result of deductive reasoning, Engels (1972) believes that the family evolved through the Consanguine family, Punaluan family, Pairing family, Monogamous family, and is trending towards Monogamous family in which there is perfect equality in the treatment of male and female.

Westermarck (1901) defines marriage as "a more or less durable connection between male and female, lasting beyond the mere act of propagation till after the birth of the offspring" (p. 537) in support of his claim that there was no primitive promiscuity. However, Engels (1972) rejects this definition by arguing that Westermarck (1901):

> Applies the term "marriage" to every relationship in which the two sexes remain mated until the birth of the offspring . . . this kind of marriage can very well occur under the conditions of promiscuous intercourse without contradicting the principle of promiscuity—the absence of any restriction imposed by custom on sexual intercourse. (p. 101)

The opposite view of Westermarck (1901) is predicated on his definition of marriage previously mentioned. This definition led to the assertion that close care of the children was the duty of the mother and the father was protector and provider of the family. It also suggests that the family forms the nucleus of the social group even in antiquity. Westermarck (1901) concluded that "human marriage, in all probability, is an inheritance from some ape-like progenitor" (p. 538).

Westermarck (1901) makes a distinction between promiscuity and free sexual intercourse before marriage because promiscuity "involves a suppression of individual inclinations" (p. 539). He further argued that sexual intercourse was considered impure among members of the same family or household from very early. This is supported by "the view that consanguineous marriages in some way or other are more or less detrimental to the species" (Westermarck, 1901, p. 546). The horror of incest seems to be universal on the basis of this phenomenon.

Westermarck (1901) believes that man started out with marriage by capture, which led to marriage by purchase, ceremonies and religious rites. Humans then passed on to the various forms of marriage. Westermarck (1901) concludes that the forms of marriage are polygyny and polyandry, both of which are modified in a monogamous direction. This conclusion is tenable on the basis that "among the causes by which the forms of marriage are influenced, the numerical proportion between the sexes plays an important part" (Westermarck, 1901, p. 547). In the evolution of marriage, the wife did not have much right and was considered the property of the husband in the early stages but gradually changed so that the rights of the wife have been extended, and she is no longer considered the property of her husband. There is now the idea that marriage "should be a contract on the basis of perfect equality between the sexes" (Westermarck, 1901, p. 550).

The schools of thought on the history of human marriage reviewed so far suggest that there is no conclusive evidence on the origin of human marriage as presented by sociologists. It could as well be argued that there was original promiscuity as monogamy. However, what is clear is that women were not given much right and were considered men's property or in some way subjugated to men. There was a pronounced inequality of the sexes guided by the patriarchal religious understanding which we will now examine.

On the theological side of the coin, there are also divergent views. Hove (1999) contends that "over the past thirty years a great debate has raged regarding the roles of men and women" (p. 15). This debate is waged at two basic levels: sexual roles and equality. However, centuries before, these were not issues to be debated because it was established that there were clear roles for men and women and the sexes could not be seen as equal. The current socio-economic situation gives rise to the complementarian and egalitarian views in opposition to the patriarchal understanding which stood for centuries.

In relation to the theological debate on the equality of the sexes, many turn to Galatians 3:28 (Hove, 1999). In applying the Galatians text, Boomsma (1993) notes that unity in Christ is the basis for equality. However, it is argued by Hove (1999) that the context of this passage is about oneness not about equality. Hove (1999) observes that "egalitarians usually start with some sense of 'equality' or 'spiritual equality' derived from Galatians 3:28 and conclude with the denial of gender-based roles in the home and church" (p. 144). There are others who argue for equality, citing Genesis chapters 1 and 2 (Bilezikian, 1985). The question about the nature of female-male relationship as originally intended by God must be answered from the first two chapters of Genesis (Bilezikian, 1985).

The presupposition of this theological discussion on the origin of marriage is tied to the origin of man. It is believed that man was created by God; he did not evolve from some ape. "The beginnings of human history are correlated to the beginnings of time itself, and human life is described as the glorious culmination of God's creative endeavours" (Bilezikian, 1985, p. 21). A relevant theological understanding of the issue of equality and marriage must start in Genesis chapter 1:26–28 (Benton, 2000). Genesis chapter 1 presents Man as a being created by God as both male and female. There was no difference in their creation and subsequently no difference in the dominion given to them by God. "The lack of any restrictions or of any qualifications in their participation in the task implies roles of equality for man and woman" (Bilezikian, 1985, p. 24).

The creation narrative in Genesis chapter 2 is often referred to as the second Creation story. It is possible that this account is a redaction of Genesis chapter 1. This claim is augmented by the statement "Therefore a man leaves his father and his mother and cleaves to his wife, and they become one flesh" (Genesis 2:24) because this seems to be the author's application of the previous verses (Bilezikian, 1985). Although there are questions regarding the literal interpretation of this passage, Bilezikian (1985) claims that:

> The teachings of the second chapter of Genesis confirm and expand upon those of chapter 1. They provide a rationale for the essential unity of human nature in male and female. They also show that in God's creation ideal, man and woman were expected to enjoy a relationship of mutuality in equality. There is nothing in Genesis 1 and 2 that provides even a hint of a disparity of nature or rank between man and woman. (p. 36–37)

The traditional view, which is grounded in patriarchy, has been argued from passages such as 1 Corinthians 11 and 14, Colossians 3, Ephesians 5, 1 Timothy 2, and 1 Peter 3. In this traditional perspective, there is a hierarchy between male and female, which is ordained by God from Creation. This hierarchy is applicable to marriage and the family from the perspective of those who argue for the traditional view (Kroeger and Beck, 1996). Man is placed at the top with authority over woman. There are specific roles in marriage with a bias towards man being leader and woman as submissive follower. The man has the final say in decision-making and the woman is primarily responsible to stay home and take care of the family while the man is primarily the breadwinner (Kroeger and Beck, 1996).

The presupposition of a Creator who created man as male and female suggests equality in the joint task to have dominion and to procreate in a regulated sexual relationship. On the basis that God created man and woman, not men and women, it is tenable that monogamy was the order of things because those who procreated would follow the pattern of those created to relate sexually.

The patriarchal system came in as a result of man's sin against his Creator, and a part of the punishment of woman was man ruling over her (Gen. 3:16), which changed the course of things. This caused the suppression of women by men and cases of polygamy. Even in this patriarchal landscape, there were women in antiquity who were in high standing (Arlandson, 1997). These cases of women in high social standing suggest that male dominance was imposed and not intrinsic.

Scripture passages have been used to create tension between female subordination and equality (Keener, 1992). Kroeger and Beck (1996) note that "teachings that cause both women and men to mistrust and despise femininity damage and diminish all of us" (p. 27). The reality of the struggle of women under a patriarchal system over the centuries and the need for a paradigm shift is captured well by Hurley's (1981) observation that "the twentieth century has seen a revolution in the relation of women and men. Women have been 'liberated' from the status of 'second-class' citizens" (p. 17).

3

The Historicity of Marriage

THE TASK OF TRACING the development of the family is a challenging one for two main reasons: it is clear that the family has mushroomed; and modern man was not there from the beginning to observe what took place. However, archaeological evidence, along with historical and other records, can help us to establish some salient points about the evolution of the family. Gillette and Reinhardt (1942) succinctly state that "the history of the family is largely a history of the attitudes of the sexes toward each other" (p. 549). This implies that a proper treatment of the history of the family needs to be guided by how the sexes related over the centuries.

It is evident that we have not moved from civilization as we know it to another stage of civilization. Covey (2004) recognizes that we have moved from the Hunter Age all the way through to the Information Age. Gillette and Reinhardt (1942) state that "in order to have an intelligent view of the family, it is necessary to think of it as an institution that has evolved out of human experience" (p. 549). The question that confronts us, therefore, is how have the experiences of the sexes shaped the family through the centuries? To help answer this question, it is important to look at how the family has been conceptualized by anthropologists, ethnologists, historians and sociologists.

Morgan (as cited in Lewis Henry Morgan, 2008), an American ethnologist and a principal founder of scientific anthropology in the nineteenth century, identifies three distinct periods in human history—savagery, barbarism and civilization. The term savagery and barbarism must not be interpreted based on their negative connotations. The intention is to be objectively descriptive, not to conjure up offensive imagery. Morgan (as cited in Talmey, 1938) presents humanity's advancement through the stages as follows:

1. Savagery—which has three stages—in stage one, human beings lived in trees and caves in warm climates and ate fruits. In stage two they moved in hordes in colder climates and discovered fire and added fish to their diet. In stage three they invented bow for hunting and added animal food to their diet.
2. Barbarism—which has three stages—in stage one, they invented pottery. In stage two they started to engage in agriculture. In stage three they discovered metal.
3. Civilization—characterized by a more advanced society in agriculture.

It is argued that each of these stages in human advancement brought about concurrent changes in the attitudes of the sexes towards each other and how they consequently related. Therefore, human beings' attitudes were shaped by their discoveries and experiences. These periods of human history will help in understanding the dynamics in the family through the centuries from the perspective of evolution. We will return to how the stages shape marriage and human experiences anon.

Studies conducted by sociologist Murdock (as cited in Haralambos and Holborn, 1995) reveal that the concept of family is a universal principle and an inevitable social institution.

There are variations in family structures across cultures, ranging from the nuclear family with mother and father living with their children, to the extended family with mother and father living with their children and their own parents or siblings. There is also a mixture of family structures even within a particular culture. In the Caribbean, for example, the family forms include nuclear, single parent, matrifocal, patrifocal, extended, blended and sibling family systems (Watson and Davidson, 2006).

Dunlap (1935) asserts that "historically, the family has been an ever changing structure, and its functions have changed in accordance with the physical and social conditions in which the family had been organized" (p. 134). This implies that the functions of the family are susceptible to change over time. According to sociologists, the family has some key functions across societies. Dunlap (1935) notes the following functions of the family through the passage of time:

1) The genetic function - rearing children, a part of this is the reproduction function.

2) The economic and marital functions—the sustenance of life and the sexual function, which has to do with providing for the physical needs of the family members (food, clothing, and shelter) and fulfilling the sexual needs of the couple.

3) The educational function—the responsibility for what the child learns.

4) The political function—rules and responsibilities decided by the family.

5) The religious function—the family was responsible for the religious education of the child.

6) The psychological function—meeting emotional needs through love and affection. It includes developing securely attached children. Children develop healthy self-concept and self-esteem through words of affirmation and positive reinforcement. Couples are also empowered to be themselves around each other without fear of rejection.

For some societies, the functions of the family include only the genetic, sexual, educational and economic aspects. It should be noted that changes have impacted these functions. For example, the educational function has been impacted by public school and peers; the political function by government; the religious function by the church; and the psychological function by the media. However, the sexual function is a common feature across cultures (Dunlap, 1935).

Although some sociologists have refuted Murdock's claim (as cited in Haralambos and Holborn, 1995), the family seems to be the rule rather than the exception because the definitions articulated by sociologists converge on a number of concepts. The marriage phenomenon is of paramount importance among the concepts discussed. Murdock (as cited in Haralambos and Holborn, 1995) defines the family as a social group characterized by common residence, economic co-operation and reproduction. It includes adults of both sexes, at least two of whom maintain a socially approved sexual relationship, and one or more children, own or adopted, of the sexually cohabiting adults (p. 317).

From Murdock's perspective, the family includes adults of both sexes who engage in sexual relations based on approved social norms. This acknowledges that adults who come together for the purpose of sexual relation do so based on cultural expectations. Throughout centuries, cross-culturally, marriages have been the basis for regulating sexual cohabitation or behavior. The fact that a sexual revolution occurred in Western society supports this conclusion as well as the changing social roles (Baron and Byrne, 2000). The changes in social roles strengthen the economic position of women through career advancement and education. Dual-career family and the liberation of women through the Women's Movement ushered in a new theological understanding of the equality of the sexes. These changes suggest that the precedent was set against the continuation of a patriarchal modus operandi that is incompatible with the intrinsic nature of the sexes.

Marriage is important for the constitution of a family. Although a marriage may not constitute a family, a family cannot be constituted without a marriage (Dunlap, 1935). Therefore, it is reasonable to affirm that a discussion of the history of marriage is really a discussion about the attitude of the sexes towards each other.

A closer look at the history of marriage is imperative at this point, given the fact that Murdock's definition (as cited in Haralambos and Holborn, 1995, p. 317) has been disputed by some persons such as Hannerz, Gonzalez, Gans, and Morgan (as cited in Haralambos and Holborn, 1995). Talmey (1938) reasons that "simultaneously with humanity's advance from the lower to the higher stages [savagery, barbarism, and civilization], the relations of the sexes also changed. This is best seen by the study of the evolution of sexual morality, or the history of marriage" (p. 428). The history of marriage is therefore linked to the stages of human advancement aforementioned.

In examining the work of Morgan, the ninth century American ethnologist, Talmey (1938) noticed that marriage progressed from promiscuity to monogamy. The following stages have been observed in the progression, according to Talmey (1938):

1. Promiscuity—there were promiscuous relationships in the first stage of savagery and the males protected the females and their offspring.

2. Consanguineous family—in the second stage of savagery, there was intermarriage of brothers and sisters, and certain marriages were considered immoral, like marriage between parents and children. There was endogamy with specific restrictions.

3. Punaluan family—there was no longer intermarriage in the same clan, and the marriage of brothers and sisters was considered immoral or incestuous in the third stage of savagery. There was now the intermarriage of many sisters to each other's husbands or many brothers to each other's wives in a group. In this kind of family, the children do not know their father but know their mother's brother, who is responsible for taking care of them. Family inheritance passed through the line of the female and matriarchy prevailed.

4. Communal marriage—there was the marriage between single men and women, but there was no exclusive cohabitation right in the first stage of barbarism. Marriage was exogamous but group marriage was impossible. The male is the one that normally leaves his clan and marries in another clan. However, in biblical history, it is the female that leaves her clan. Upon his death, the husband's personal property had to be sent back to his own clan, but the main fortune remained with the clan of his wife. Housekeeping was done in a communal spirit by the females and the males provided food and fought the battles of the clan.

5. Matriarchy prevailed and kinship was traced in the female line. The theory of women being in control has been abandoned as it has been demonstrated that lineage has little to do with dominance of either sex because in all known family structures the males have control (Dunlap, 1935). Some still believe that anthropological, archaeological and historical evidence suggests that patriarchy was not a natural universal order (Johnson, 1997). However, it seems logical even from early biblical times that the balance tips in the direction of patriarchy.

6. Patriarchal family—there was required strict fidelity from the wife. During the second stage of barbarism new sources of wealth were discovered, which included the training or breeding of animals. In order to prevent the wealth (flocks and herds) of the husband from being given back to the husband's clan upon his death, family kinship was then traced in the line of the male. The male then

became ruler. In the third stage of barbarism, the father had to know his children in order for the inheritance to be passed on to the children. Therefore, strict female fidelity was a necessity.

7. Monogamous marriage—the marriage of single couples from different tribes with exclusive cohabitation made the transition into civilization. Chastity was not just a virtue but a necessity.

This history of marriage illustrates that the family was structured through the centuries based on how sexual relationships were regulated. Therefore, Murdock's definition of the functions of the family might be very well grounded. Many have disputed this claim of primitive promiscuity, and there is widespread disagreement among the historians of marriage as to the first form of human marriage. Noted among them is The argument of Westermarck, the Finnish sociologist, philosopher, and anthropologist, who published his influential book, *The History of Human Marriage* in 1891. The argument of Westermarck (1901) emphatically debunks the widely accepted view that early human beings had originally lived in a state of promiscuity. He postulates that monogamy was the original form of sexual attachment among humans.

Westermarck (1901) diametrically opposed an original state of promiscuity, as human beings did not adopt to monogamy through experience but were inclined to relate in this way by nature. It means that human sexual experience has not merely evolved but was regulated by natural inclination towards monogamy. The observation that the sexes are almost always equal gives some credence to this view.

Morgan (1877) or Engels' (1972) interpretation of Morgan in his book *The Origin of the Family, Private Property and the State* seems consistent with an evolutionary perspective on human beings and marriage. This view is based on the presupposition that human beings evolved from some ape and passed through the stages of savagery, barbarism, and currently progressing in the civilized stage. The argument of Westermarck (1901), in *The History of Marriage*, seems to be consistent with the Creation narrative in Genesis chapter 2 of the Jewish Bible. Westermarck (1901) argued his position from an evolutionary perspective and argued against the theory of promiscuity, thus giving credence to the Creation narrative.

The Creation story might help to solve this problem of the origin of marriage. The account of Creation from a Judeo-Christian perspective dates back to 1446 BC, if Moses is credited as the author of the Pentateuch (the first five books of the Jewish and Christian Bible respectively). Many societies predate the record of the Creation story. For example, an examination of the Babylonian code of Hammurabi from 1775 BC and tablets containing Assyrian laws between 1450 and 1240 BC revealed that there was a practice of patriarchal marriage in both cultures, with women being treated as property in the Assyrian culture (Hurley, 1981). The difference between the cultures of the Assyrians and Babylonians in comparison to the Israeli culture, dating from 1800 BC, in the treatment of women, was that the former was not guided by religion. It can be concluded that the Judeo-Christian perspective on marriage, which is rooted in patriarchy, has had a profound impact on the history of marriage in Western societies.

The Creation narrative gives more credence to the view that human beings did not originally live in a state of promiscuity. From the Creation story, human beings appear to start out in regulated sexual behavior. While archaeological findings can help in understanding how humans lived, it cannot help as much in establishing how the sexes related and therefore we must depend on written records. The challenge remains because whatever evidence is available still requires a certain level of faith for its acceptance. Some of the observations do not have even a scintilla of evidence to objectively support them.

There are two main views on the subject based on our analysis. The first view is based on an evolutionary hypothesis, which either argues for a state of primitive promiscuity or primitive monogamy. The sociologists are at variance in their conclusions. The second view is based on a creation hypothesis, which argues for an original state of monogamy. There is convergence on this conclusion among theologians, although there are differences in how the second Creation narrative in Genesis chapter 2 is understood. If Westermarck's (1901) evolutionary perspective is followed, there would be convergence between some sociologists and creationists that there was never a state of promiscuity.

There are practices that could be accommodated by both the evolutionary and Creation hypotheses. These include endogamy (the practice of marrying someone from within one's own tribe or group) and exogamy (the practice of marrying outside one's group). The systems of marriage, such as exchange marriage (simultaneously giving in marriage of a male and female from one group to a male and female from another group), polyandry and polygyny will be discussed anon. However, how the sexes related to each other in terms of equality, matriarchy or patriarchy is unresolved from both the evolutionary and Creation perspectives. Notwithstanding, an historical look at religious perspectives support a patriarchal relationship from as early as evidence will allow for tracing.

Marital Systems

The conceptualization of the family as a universal social institution suggests that different marital systems exist in contemporary societies. Monogamy and polygamy are the two marital systems observed by sociologists to be predominant in societies. These systems are based on social norms within various cultures. For example, monogamy refers to the marriage of single pairs while polygamy refers to the marriage of one man to more than one woman or the marriage of one woman to more than one man. The marital systems regulate sexual behaviors in the establishment of "authentic" marriage and family systems. Ellis (1910) observes four marital systems that have been observed through the centuries cross-culturally, arising from the two original systems.

1. Monogamy—marriage of one man to one woman, which is common in Europe and other countries. This kind of marriage is believed to be the preferred approach (Dunlap, 1935; Ellis, 1910; Nisbet, 1889). It is even a necessity, given the equal number of the sexes (Nisbet, 1889; Dunlap, 1935).

2. Polygyny—refers to the marriage of one man to two or more wives simultaneously. This is practiced more in Islamic cultures. It is believed that even in these countries, where it is allowed, the great majority of the people must practice monogamy because the sexes are equal almost everywhere (Dunlap, 1935).

3. Polyandry—refers to a marriage in which one woman has several husbands simultaneously. This kind of marriage is extremely rare.

4. Group marriage—"All the women in one class are regarded as the actual, or at all events potential, wives of all the men in another class" (Ellis, 1910, p. 423). This is believed to be an extension of polyandry with the husbands of that woman having other wives.

It is acknowledged that this is rare and was at no time a dominant form of marriage (Dunlap, 1935).

It is noted that polygamy was not as common as is sometimes assumed because the sexes were always nearly equal in number. Talmey (1938) observes that "through the entire history of the polygamous Jews, about half a dozen polygamous marriages are recorded" (p. 431). However, polygamy is widely practiced now, especially in Islamic culture, which makes those who follow the Islamic faith the largest religious group that practices polygamy. Gaskiyane (2000) estimates that "over three-quarters of the world's societies permit polygamy and only 16 percent prescribe monogamy" (p. 7).

The core values in polygamous culture do not allow for an egalitarian marriage. Even the Muslim Qur'an stated in Sura 4:129 that "You cannot be equitable in a polygamous relationship, no matter how hard you try." Monogamy seems the better system of marriage because from the marital literature the practice of other marital systems would result in marital inequality. Nisbet (1889) argues:

> It is clear from our examination of the principles of heredity that the society in which the female sex is systematically downtrodden or enslaved pursues a suicidal course, and that the secret of human progress lies in the freest recognition of the rights of the individual woman. (p. 188)

This declaration is instructive because in polygamous societies, although the forms of polygamy vary, women are treated as inferior to men and are not allowed important rights and privileges. In contrast, the condition appears to be better for women in a monogamous culture. Women are allowed to marry when they want to marry and to whom they want to marry. Women seem to be valued in this kind of culture. They share public space with men and are allowed to become professionals. However, there is still a lot more to be accomplished, given the effects of our patriarchal legacy. Women need to be treated as equal in the home and family. They need to be allowed to serve in whatever way they are qualified to serve. In the same way that we do not say man president, and so on, we need to stop saying woman president, woman doctor, and so on.

Marital Decisions

The arrangement of marriage is based on cultural norms. Some cultures practice infant betrothal, where the child is given to a potential partner from birth. In Hindu marriages, child betrothal does not dissolve even at the husband's death (Nisbet, 1889). For other cultures, arranged marriages are based on the decisions of parents about whom their child will marry. These kinds of marriages are referred to as "Go-betweens Arrangements," where the conclusive point of the negotiation is the dowry or bridal gift. Marriages are seen as businesses, where parents will give their daughters in marriage without their consent, and good-looking girls are sold to wealthy men. In China, for example, a father may sell his daughter and a husband may sell his wife, and the widow's in-laws normally sell her to the highest bidder (Nisbet, 1889). In arranged marriages in the past, not even noblewomen had control over their marriages (Chambers, et al., 1999, p. 250). Finally, marriage by choice suggests that individuals will participate in the process of mate selection, dating, courtship and eventually marriage.

Polygamy is the keystone of religious traditions, such as Islam and Hinduism (Buddhism upholds the said principle). It is within these traditions that arranged marriages are still taking place. Arranged marriages do not stimulate the same kind of passion as love marriages. Research conducted by Imamoglu (as cited in Weisfeld, 1997) revealed that "arranged marriages never reach the level of "hotness" maintained in love matches, even after the so-called honeymoon period is over" (p. 362). It is believed that a successful marriage can be built only on the basis of personal respect, interest, and actual personal acquaintance (Dunlap, 1935). Therefore, a system that discriminates against women cannot do justice to the psychological development of the sexes. Polygamy continues to be a great evil, pitting the sexes against each other and treating women as inferior to men.

Balswick and Balswick (1999) conclude that throughout history, in most societies, mate selection was made by parents. In traditional marriage, love does not play an integral role as the parents choose a marriage partner for their children. However, faithfulness to one's marriage was expected in this form of arrangement (Rauch, 1998).

Free choice of marriage is a recent development. It emerged in medieval times (in the ninth century). The trend started with Pope Nicholas I in the nineteenth century and gained increasing prominence when marriage became a sacrament and a public affair in the thirteenth century. Couples were allowed to decide whether or not to accept a marriage partner through arranged marriage. The trend was set for marriage by choice, which emerged as a twentieth century phenomenon.

Free choice marriages around the world differ in the traits of chastity, domesticity and religion that one looks for in a marriage partner (Santrock, 2006). These traits are said to be motivating factors that help persons decide on whom to marry. One of the factors might play a more integral role for a particular person.

Marital decision seems to facilitate what Jung (as cited in Jones and Butman, 1991) calls the collective unconscious (all the things about the human race that continue to affect us at the unconscious level). Jones and Butman (1991) point out that "from the Jungian perspective, we are not really "in control," but are ruled by powerful transpersonal unconscious forces of which we have only limited awareness" (p. 122). This collective unconscious, grounded in our patriarchal legacy, plays a part in the practice of women being treated poorly by men. Some women continue to behave as if they have no choice and so find it more difficult to adjust in traditional marriages in relation to their sexuality than males. This observation is supported by research findings that show that marital problems are more depressing for women than men. Women tend to process relationship issues at a deeper level than men (Myers, 2005). When women are hurt, their partner is at zero in their love bank. This is part of the reason women tend to take a longer time to become sexual with their partner after an argument. In free choice marriages, within the patriarchal system, women choose their partners but are not considered or treated as equal. For example, women still have to take full responsibility for household and childrearing, even when they work outside of the home, and they have less influence on family decisions, hence the same patriarchal dominance.

Arranged marriages facilitate patriarchal dominance and so the collective unconscious continues to impact the poor treatment of women by men even in free choice marriage. Humans are being influenced by powerful forces from the past that they are not consciously aware of. Therefore, unwittingly we expect certain things from each other. This comes across in statements such as, "that is how men are" or "that is how women are." Men are accustomed to be the dominant partner and so find it difficult to share power with their wives. Our psychology of marriage is deeply embedded in the experiences of the human race. Therefore, an egalitarian marriage can be successfully built only on a clear understanding of the past and a determination to treat the sexes as equal not only in marriage but at all levels.

Based on the Genesis Creation narratives in the Jewish Bible, woman was created as man's equal. There are two accounts of the creation of man in Genesis. The account in Genesis chapter 2, patriarchal in its orientation, appears to infer that man was created before woman. Woman was created after God "recognized" that man should not be alone. However, this was not the experience of the animals; they all had a mate. However, if primal position is the basis on which man is superior, then the animals would be superior to man! If human beings are considered the crown of the Creator's creation, then woman should be placed above man. Order of creation cannot be the basis of determining dominance. Archer (1994) argues that the account in Genesis chapter 2 could be regarded as suprahistory, illustrative rather than literal.

The account in Genesis chapter 1 is in favor of an egalitarian orientation. Jesus, who is said to be from the beginning (John 1:1), gave credence to both accounts when He said in Matthew 19:4–5 "Haven't you read," he replied, "that at the beginning the Creator 'made them male and female,' and said, "For this reason a man will leave his father and mother and be united to his wife, and the two will become one flesh?" (NIV).

The response of Jesus supports the claim that Man was created as equal (male and female), the view in Genesis chapter 1 and the argument for uniting in marriage, the view in Genesis chapter 2. Jesus used the first account to talk about the creation of man and the second account to talk about the permanence of marriage. I will use the approach of Jesus because it objectively supports the egalitarian view being advocated. Munce (1985) agrees that in Genesis chapter 1 man is created as male and female. The antediluvian perspective (before Noah's flood in the Bible) in Genesis chapter 5:1–2 also supports the view that man was created as male and female. "This is the written account of Adam's line. When God created man, he made him in the likeness of God. He created them male and female and blessed them. And when they were created, he called them man" (NIV).

Marital Inequality

Throughout the centuries, the process of marriage seems to be mainly patriarchal in nature. Johnson (1997) proposes that "a society is patriarchal to the degree that it is male dominated, male-identified, and male-centered. It also involves as one of its key aspects the oppression of women" (p. 5). Patriarchy is a legacy to which we are collectively tied in a knot, where men are in the foreground and women in the background. Language in a patriarchal society is male biased. Even men, who are not "powerful," gain personal power by just being male (Johnson, 1997). Women who have the potential to become "powerful" remain powerless because they are women. They are left to feel disappointed that they are female and not male.

Patriarchy is seen even in the fact that polyandry is extremely rare. The role(s) of women is seen as mainly homemaking and satisfying the sexual needs of men even without their own enjoyment of the sex act. The subordination of women is not so much because of their connection with their children (childrearing responsibility) but their connection with men (Johnson, 1997). Wives and children were even treated like property. This negative treatment of women is seen in the kind of employment that they were able to obtain and the salary that they were able to earn. Marriages were based more on segregated conjugal roles than joint conjugal roles (Haralambos and Holborn, 1995).

In looking at the history of marriage, one can see how degrading it has been for women. Women were probably initially free as men, if the concept of matriarchy, discussed earlier, is accepted. What is very clear is that women later became the property of their husbands in the third stage of savagery (Engels, 1972). They could be purchased like other commodities (Dunlap, 1935). The rise of slavery also aided this degrading treatment of women. A slave master would inevitably have sexual relations with the woman he purchased and could rent her at will. The emphasis on female chastity, without the same for males, served to further subjugate women. The chastity of women was geared at facilitating the exclusive right of men to their "property." The emphasis on female virginity was not for the purpose of containing population growth but for reinforcing male dominance. It was appropriate for a man to have sex with an unmarried woman. A man could divorce his wife but a wife could not divorce her husband until recently.

The conditions of women under these circumstances were grossly inhumane. There was the sale of wife and wife swapping. A woman's place was in the home, and the best a woman could hope for was to be sold as a bride to a good suitor, who could cause her to live in luxury, without labor as the price for her sexual favors (Dunlap, 1935). The conditions of women left them economically dependent on men and at the mercy of men. This is captured well by (Dunlap, 1935) in the observation that:

> Until recently, woman had but two vocations open to her, both involving her sale or rental of herself, or her sale or rental by male owners. On account of her rapid decline in value with age, the best bargain for her was sale as a wife. Prostitution, her only other possibility, was a poor business arrangement so far as she was concerned. Her chances of being a wife depending upon her virginity, and the permanence of the bargain upon her chastity, these conditions were enforced upon women with comparative ease. (pp. 174, 175)

Economic independence of women overtime has revolutionized marriage (Dunlap, 1935). Without economic independence women seem to have no power and even with some economic independence women still struggle to be seen and treated as equal.

Amidst the effort of the Feminist Movement and the changes in the workforce, which allow women to work outside the home, inequality continues in marriages. Schwartz (1998) supports this reality in her conclusion that "Despite several decades of dissecting the sexism and inequality inherent in traditional marriage . . . we have yet to develop a clear picture of how more balanced marital partnerships actually work" (p. 84). Egalitarianism is not automatic even in dual-career relationships. There is a dire need to resist the temptation of allowing money to determine who has more power.

Inequality in marriage has been studied from the perspective of the allocation of domestic responsibility and distribution of power between husband and wife. Some sociologists have argued that conjugal roles are becoming equal; others have maintained that inequality is not significantly reduced. In studies conducted in Britain, sociologists concluded that women are far from acquiring equality with men. Women are still primarily responsible for domestic responsibility and they have less power than men in their marriages (Haralambos and Holborn, 1995). A spouse's (usually the husband) unwillingness to share power is often seen in bad marriages, at least in Western cultures (Santrock, 2006). A new paradigm is needed in order to build a successful marriage in an age that is characterized by divorce. Egalitarianism needs to replace patriarchism in order to shake the controlling patriarchal paradigm. There is the thinking that women are inferior to men and women are merely attachments to men in marriage so men decide how women should be treated and women have no say in the matter.

Theological Impacts on Marriage

There is a unique relationship between religion and culture through which culture influences religion just as religion influences culture. The impact of religion on culture is determined by a number of factors. In many societies, religion plays an integral role in the function of marriage. The religious understanding of a person influences her or his life in significant ways, including the shaping of marital attitudes. There is relative fluidity in the influence of religion on attitudes because empirical evidence indicates that cognition and emotions do not necessarily parallel each other (Baucom, 2001). That is, people do not necessarily practice their religious beliefs. However, it is clear that religion has a powerful impact on peoples' attitudes and behaviors because culture and religion influence each other.

The religious systems of Islam, Buddhism and Hinduism continue to impact negatively on the lives of women through the practice of polygamy. Women are treated as inferior to men, and the core value of the family structure is the production of children. The production of children, as a part of the reproductive cycle, appears more valuable than the actual marriage relationship. The veiling of women and the separation of the sexes as a form of social control also affect the psychological development of the women. For example, it reinforces male dominance and female inferiority, where women believe they are at the mercy of men. In addition, men behave as if women belong to them and so a justification for poor treatment is warranted. Women are made to think that they have no choice. Dunlap (1935) asserts the need for proper relationship between the sexes in his observation that "the proper setting for both . . . is many friendships of moderate intimacy, until one finally ripens fully" (p. 168). This kind of treatment is facilitated in a monogamous culture.

The religious practice of separating the sexes is a low form of civilization because women continue to be treated as inferior to men.

Civilization connotes respect for human life and dignity. Dunlap (1935) concurs that "social separation of the sexes, unchastity before marriage, purchasing of wives, and 'arranged' marriages, therefore, tend to a low order of civilization, and fundamental social progress is away from them" (p. 169). It goes without saying that where women continue to be treated as inferior, social progress will be retarded. Therefore, any religion that promotes this continues to promote evil against humanity.

It is sometimes believed that Christianity is responsible for the introduction of monogamy. Monogamy was not introduced based on the concept of sexual sin. The historians of marriage, as noted earlier, concluded that it resulted out of human experience, and there is a human tendency towards monogamy, even if only on the basis that the numbers of the sexes are almost equal. High morality was already present in the later Roman Empire as it relates to sexuality before the beginning of the Christian era (Ellis, 1910; Nisbet, 1889). In biblical history, given the fact that polygamy was practiced by the patriarchs and sanctioned by Moses, if high morality was present in the Roman Empire during the advent of Christianity it simply means that Christianity fell on fertile soil, with the emphasis that a man should have only one wife until death.

The Christian religion understood marriage in many different ways through the centuries. In the early stages, childbearing in every situation was regarded as sinful. Women were seen as instruments of Satan. Celibacy was promoted through monasteries and nunneries and second marriages were viewed as abominable. Married women could not approach the altar or touch the Eucharist. It was doubtful whether married couples cohabiting together could be saved. Couples were encouraged to avoid sexual intercourse. Restriction was placed on the marriage of priests. Marriage ceremonies had to be performed by a priest in order for the marriage to be binding. Sexual desire was seen as the lower side of human beings with some shame attached to it and women were treated like slaves or cattle in some places (Nisbet 1889). The imposition of oppressive religious dogma painted a negative picture of Christianity in relation to marriage. Ellis (1910) notes that the first fifteen hundred years of Christianity's reign "represents on the whole the most degraded condition to which the marriage system has ever been known to fall for so long a period during the whole course of human history" (p. 430). However, Christianity is responsible for evolving marriage from a simple private agreement between a man and woman to "a public contract."

It is also responsible for making it easy to enter marriage but difficult to abandon a marital commitment (Ellis, 1910). Christianity has influenced the European law of monogamy and the morality of it (Nisbet, 1889). Therefore, unlike Islam, Buddhism and Hinduism, Christianity has done a lot for the liberation of women (Nisbet, 1889).

Through the centuries, the role of women in the church, marriage and family has been understood in various ways, with a bias towards male dominance. In recent times, especially in the West, a new theological understanding of women has surfaced. The revision of theology suggests sociological shifts, which allow women to work outside the home and even to delay marriage until later in life. Carter and Peters (1998) reason that "partly because of economics and partly because of the women's movement, women's behavior has changed drastically since the sixties. . . . But men's behavior has changed far less" (p. 176). There needs to be a paradigm shift from the controlling mindset of patriarchy to the liberating mindset of egalitarianism. There is no rhyme or reason for women to be held in perpetual bondage. Modern man is not exculpated from responsibility for keeping women in perpetual bondage on the basis of our patriarchal legacy and the power of the collective unconscious.

The history of marriage suggests that a patriarchal paradigm is responsible for pitting the sexes against each other. The result of this paradigm is seen in the phenomenal divorce rate in this generation due to socio-cultural shifts. In order to combat this constant threat of divorce, there needs to be a new way of thinking and being. An egalitarian paradigm seems to be the way forward because it allows for a new way of thinking and being that encourages equality of the sexes in all areas of life and human endeavors.

4

Common Problems and Reasons for Marital Failure

MYERS (2005) INDICATES THAT happily married people live longer. He further notes that married people of both sexes report being more happy than single (never married), divorced, or separated persons (p. 600). Therefore, if we are able to discover what makes persons happily married, the opposite would be true for what makes them unhappy in their marriages. Issues that contribute to marital unhappiness are common problems associated with marriage.

Commitment seems to be an important factor in marital satisfaction because it reflects the degree to which marital partners are interested in maintaining the success of their marriages. The nature of one's commitment will affect the duration of intimate relationships (Frank and Brandstätter, 2002). Adams and Jones (1997) used research findings to support their conclusion that marital commitment is defined many different ways among writers. They postulate that commitment within the marital process has three components:

1. An attraction component, which is based on personal dedication, devotion, and love;

2. A moral component, which is based on one's sense of obligation, religious integrity, or social responsibility;

3. A constraining component, which is based on fear of the social, financial, or legal consequences of relationship termination (p. 1190).

The researchers conducted six studies on commitment to support their conclusion and suggest that an analysis of the commitment construct implies that marital problems are as a result of poor attitudes, poor morals and self-centeredness. The three components of commitment as described above are germane to marital satisfaction. An absence of the components within the marriage system will result in marital dissatisfaction.

Santrock (2006) maintains that "Gottman's research [since the early 1970s] represents the most extensive assessment of marital relationships available" (p. 483). In Gottman's research (as cited in Santrock, 2006) the following seven principles determine the success of a marriage:

1. Establishing love maps
2. Nurturing fondness and admiration
3. Turning towards each other instead of away
4. Letting your partner influence you
5. Solving solvable conflicts
6. Overcoming gridlock
7. Creating shared meaning

In contrast to the seven principles to make a successful marriage, there will be marital problems when one fails to treat one's partner as special. Further, lack of appreciation, enmity, power struggle, lack of self-control, impatience and lack of joint goal setting and working towards goal accomplishments are negative factors which contribute to marital problems.

Whisman, Dixon and Johnson (1997), although their study should be viewed with caution due to methodology, suggest that the top five common marital problems are "lack of loving feelings, power struggles, communication, affairs, and unrealistic expectations" (p. 363). The marital problems in the study are based on composite rankings to support the issue of power, communication and unrealistic expectations. Marital problems, including lack of love, power struggle, communication difficulties, affairs, and unrealistic expectations could be viewed as a reluctance to adopt the appropriate attitudes and behaviors.

Collins (1988) argues that marital problems include faulty communication, under-integrated or over-integrated relationships, interpersonal tensions (including sex, inflexibility, roles, religion, values, conflicting needs, personality differences and money), external pressures and boredom. Storaasli and Markman (1990) assert that the literature on marital problems dates back to the 1920s and continues to provide evidence that most couples face typical problems in the course of their marriages. These problem areas include sex, money, relatives, communication, affection, children, recreation, leisure, friends, jealousy, alcohol or drugs, and religion. Christian and psychological viewpoints support the fact that most couples encounter a wide range of marital problems in order to sustain their relationships. Storaasli and Markman (1990) affirm that "the inability of marital partners to cope with their problems has been viewed as one of the most powerful factors contributing to marital dissatisfaction, if not the most prominent cause of marital dissolution" (p. 81).

Human sexuality needs to be clearly understood. Sexuality is very complex. It is what we are and involves what we do. It includes the cultural concept of gender as well as the concept of sex, female and male. It has more to do with how one feels about what he or she does than what one actually does. It includes a person's basic identity (Firestone, Firestone, and Catlett, 2006).

Marriages are blighted from a lack of discussion of the issue of sexuality. A discussion of sexuality is important because one's sexuality is controlled or influenced by multiple factors including genetic, environmental, social, cultural, and religious, which suggests that many things can tarnish one's sexual identity. Awareness is crucial for healthy sexual identity formation. There is no need to be ashamed of one's sexuality but a willingness to explore and discover who one really is as an individual and in relation to one's spouse. Failure to understand human sexuality can result in serious marital problems. For example, if one does not first "own" him or herself, one will have a challenge to give him or herself to another in marriage because one has to first own something before he or she can give it to another. Ownership of self is a prerequisite for giving self (Covey, 1989, 2004).

The issue of sex as a major marital distracter seems to have far-reaching effects on marriages. Amatory satisfaction is an important aspect of the marital relationship and must never be underestimated. There are many sexual dysfunctions that can affect a marriage. These include sexual desire disorders (absent or low sexual interest or no desire and avoidance and aversion to sexual intercourse), sexual arousal disorders, orgasmic disorders, and sexual pain disorders (Sue, Sue, and Sue, 1997). Therefore, one should be aware of the possibility of sexual issues that may need to be addressed to increase marital satisfaction.

Although trends affirm that sex-roles are changing, marital issues raised in therapy suggest that attitudes, especially related to men are not changing because of the penetrating effects of patriarchy. Men seem to merely accept women working outside the home mainly for economic reasons (Carter and Peters, 1998). Society seems to be trapped in the patriarchal legacy, which is characterized by the unceasing oppression of women.

There is a continuous debate on the issue of personality traits in marriage. A review of the marriage literature suggests that the needs of men differ from those of women (Gray, 1992; Harley, 1997). Conflict in marriage can be seen as the result of two competing need systems (Clinebell, 1984). For example, men and women may speak the same or different love language (Chapman, 2004) and women and men's attitude reflects differences towards money (Dakin and Wampler, 2008). The literature review proves that there are certain levels of difference in personality, temperament, and even religious understanding. Research suggests that "similarity between partners' personalities may not be closely tied to marital happiness" (Gattis, et al., 2004, p. 564). There is supporting empirical data for the claim that marriages can be healthy even when there are differences in personality.

In comparison to personality differences, commitment seems vital in building a healthy marriage (Adams and Jones, 1997). Personality characteristics, such as neuroticism and impulse control, are strongly correlated to marital stability and satisfaction (Kelley and Conley, 1987). Therefore, diverse factors, such as commitment, personality, sex-roles, sex and sexuality, contribute to both marital success and marital problems. It is very important for marital problems to be dealt with because they can cause "depression, obsessive thoughts, sexual dysfunction, inability to work effectively, difficulty in making new friends, and self-condemnation" (Santrock, 2006, p. 475). A successful marriage requires (among other things) honesty, integrity, fair play, dedication, generosity, maturity and flexibility (Schwartz, 1998).

Markhman, Halford and Lindahl (2000) state that Western cultures have more than 90 percent of the population marrying by the age of 50 and most of the individuals who decide not to marry are involved in marriage-like relationships (p. 110). It is important to note that while marriage is the norm in Western cultures, marital dissolution is very high and concomitant with the onset of social changes within societies. The social changes are as follows: 1) the number of women working outside of the home; 2) a more accepting attitude towards divorce; 3) changes in divorce laws; 4) increased geographical mobility of couples; 5) reduced contacts with extended family; 6) the acceptance of homosexual marriages in some areas; 7) advancement in technology (Markhman, et al., 2000). Increased cohabitation of males and females has also impacted negatively on marriage rates, resulting in persons delaying marriage (Crary, 2007).

A failure of one or both partners to separate from family of origin can cause a marriage to fail. It is therefore very important for couples to complete the psychological task of separating from family of origin from very early in their marriage. Wallerstein (1994) argues that:

> Psychological separation from the family of origin is a formidable achievement for men and women alike, so much so that a significant number of failed young marriages appear to represent unsuccessful efforts by one or both partners to separate from an emotionally disturbed family of origin (efforts that often lead to a perpetuation of the psychopathology that the young person sought to escape). (p. 643)

Social changes have ushered in a transformation of the marital relationship, where a new attitudinal style signals a departure from traditional gender roles and transfer of power to a more pervasive egalitarian relationship of role-flexibility and equality. Social change, which aids in the transformation of the marital relationship, can sometimes generate conflicts of career, childrearing, finances and consensus of opinion. The relative evolution of the marital structure creates significant strain on a marital relationship if not carefully managed. Despite rapid progress, we nevertheless continue to be shackled by our collective patriarchal legacy.

Difficulties in Marriage

A plethora of issues forms part of the marriage relationship as a result of social changes which may or may not lead to dissolution of the marriage. However, many problems, such as power struggle, unfair expectations, poor communication and lack of commitment, may be cited as precipitating causes to marital difficulties. There is empirical evidence to suggest that marriage partners "identified a number of sources of marital conflict, including lack of satisfaction, stubbornness and withdrawal from interaction, defensiveness, and negative emotional expression" (Enright and Fitzgibbons, 2000, p. 195). Mudd (1963) suggests that these difficulties can be summed up as a lack of consideration on the part of one partner for the other. Markhman et al. (2000) report that:

> [Marital] relationship within social-learning perspectives suggests that couples begin their relationship happily and that levels of love and attraction are eroded by the negative way partners often treat each other as they negotiate the stress and conflict that inevitably occurs in relationships. (p. 111)

The conclusion to be drawn from Markhman's (2000) perspective is that a lack of consideration or a negative way of relating will include affection and sex, monetary concerns, work or recreation, unmet preconceived ideas on spousal roles, undesirable individual differences and ineffective communication. Mudd (1963) concludes that "the basic complaint is that a person fails to consider his [or her] spouse's feelings, needs, values, and goals, or acts in disregard of them" (p. 965). This can also be seen as failure to reciprocate love (Santrock, 2006).

A closer look at some of the specific factors noted above are attributed to marital failure and would warrant further analysis of issues related to family of origin, communication difficulties, personality issues, intimacy issues, emotional instability, religious differences, unresolved problems, conflict manage deficiencies, lack of commitment, problems of attachment, lack of self-disclosure and love.

Communication is the glue that holds a relationship together for which Markhman et al. (2000) noted that the problem of communication is considered the most frequently cited complaint by 90 percent of couples seeking therapy (p. 112). This indicates that ineffectual communication may be a major factor in marital breakdown, as communication patterns tend to deteriorate with marital distress due to couples' hostilities, demanding change of the other partner, a failure to listen actively, withdrawal, being emotionally reactive, negativity in day-to-day interaction and behavioral bias (Markhman, et al., 2000). In troubled relationships, the presence of the other partner in the marital cycle is associated with pain and an obstacle to pleasure. Dysfunctional marital relationships are significant barriers to effective communication. Scott and Castellani (2002) note that the maintenance of an affective tone in couple relationships may be a trajectory to successful relationship(s).

The construct of personality similarity is crucial for marital success. Bentler and Newcomb (1978) discovered from a longitudinal study that when personality traits are homogeneous at the onset of marriage, marital success is more likely. The findings further allude that if there is no similarity in personality trait, marital failure is more likely. Although this study was conducted two decades ago, the researchers predicted that their study would not be significantly affected by social changes in society. Social changes do not affect the significance of homogeneous personality traits as a predictor of marital success. The research findings are corroborated by Baron and Byrne (2000) whose recent study indicates "similar attitudes arouse positive affect and dissimilar attitudes arouse negative affect . . . and affect influences attraction" (p. 291). From an analysis of the two empirical research findings, there needs to be a level of congeniality among marriage partners.

Dissatisfaction with the type and level of intimacy in the relationship can cause a marriage to fail. Devine and Forehand (1996) conducted a study which suggests that marital satisfaction prevented divorce. Intimacy is important because each partner within a marriage may perceive intimacy differently. Tolstedt and Stokes (1983) studied intimacy in marital satisfaction and concluded the following, that verbal intimacy, affective intimacy and physical intimacy are all important components to marital satisfaction. When verbal and affective intimacies are high, even if physical intimacy is low, it will not be a problem. A marriage will fail when self-disclosure is narrow, shallow and the level of interaction between the couple is negative. A marriage is likely to fail due to an absence of feelings of closeness, emotional bonding and support, which may impact physical intimacy.

If one or both partners are emotionally unstable, the marriage could fail due to unresolved issues from the family of origin resulting in marital strain (Wallerstein, 1994). Unresolved issues, as a psychological task of marriage, have been shown to affect one's ability to deal appropriately with conflicts, poor attitudes, and areas of intimacy, which are important components for marital satisfaction. Unresolved issues are further responsible for poor attitudes and engagement in actions that are destructive to marriage as a result of low self-esteem and relationship insecurities (Cook and Douglas, 1998).

Misplaced religiosity could lead to marriage failure. Mahoney, Pargament, Tarakeshwar, and Swank (as cited in Baucom, 2001) note that most married couples living in the United States are religious, and have beliefs that faith has an important influence. Fiese and Tomcho (as cited in Baucom, 2001) opine that the meaning of religious rituals were more important for husbands while the actual practice of the ritual was more important for wives. Conflict over religious rituals is an important tenet, given the different perspectives of the couple. Religious values can positively affect commitment to the marriage. Baucom (2001) affirms that "the introduction of children into the family often serve as a strong stimulus for couples to address religious and spiritual issues, because their decisions are likely to affect the children in addition to the couple" (p. 655). This affirmation suggests that religiosity can have either a negative or positive impact on marriage.

Unresolved conflicts and poor conflict management skills are often the causes for failed marriages. Given the decision to share space and give up personal freedom(s), intimate relationships can create a level of tension. However, the degree of tension will determine whether or not a conflict develops. Marital conflicts can be very deep emotionally, and it is important that couples strive to create a stress-free atmosphere in their marriage. Frequency and seriousness of conflicts are positively correlated with marital atmosphere (Lewin, 1997). Davey, Fincham, Beach, and Brody (2001) argue that marital conflict results when causal attribution leads to responsible attribution, which implies that when couples blame each other for what is happening conflicts tend to arise. One could conclude that if a couple shares responsibility for strengthening the relationship, then conflicts will not intensify.

A lack of commitment within a marriage can be manifested in power struggle, due to unrealistic expectations, infidelity, abuse, inflexibility, and an unwillingness to forgive and hence marital failure. One's commitment to protect the marriage is based on an egalitarian attitude in order to prevent power struggles and unrealistic expectations, due to lack of open communication, from negatively affecting the relationship.

Finally, researchers have documented factors that predict marital success, such as attachment, equity, self-disclosure, and love (Myers, 2005; Feldman, 2005). According to Myers (2005) marriage usually endures if the person(s):

- married after age 20.
- both grew up in stable, two-parent homes.

- dated for a long while before marriage.
- are well and similarly educated.
- enjoy a stable income from a good job.
- live in a small town or on a farm.
- did not cohabit or become pregnant before marriage.
- are religiously committed.
- are of a similar age, faith, and education. (pp. 468–469)

These factors are considered important in individualistic cultures like the United States of America, and the conclusion can be drawn that none of these factors stands on its own in order to build a lasting marriage. Failing the prerequisites, then marital failure is almost inevitable (Myers, 2005).

Culture can also contribute to marital failure, where cultural value systems have significant impact. Myers (2005) reports that "divorce rates varied widely by country, ranging from .01 percent of the population annually in Bolivia, the Philippines, and Spain to 4.7 percent in the world's most divorce-prone country, the United States" (p. 468). In North America about 50 percent of marriages end in divorce.

Statistics indicate that individualistic cultures have higher divorce rates than collectivist cultures. In individualistic cultures, such as the United States of America, marriage is based on the concept of "as long as we love each other" and marriage is not viewed as a permanent arrangement. Commitment in a relationship may be broken if the perception of unmet needs is prevalent in the marriage relationship.

The fickleness of the marriage commitment may be strengthened by the fact that sometimes persons choose to marry for the wrong reason. For example, in communal culture, the concept is "as long as we both live" which suggests a permanent arrangement. Marital commitment is more important than perceived personal fulfillment, which is reinforced by research that affirmed that love is a necessary ingredient in marriage in individualistic cultures. In collectivist cultures, such as China and South Africa, love is not internalized as a necessary ingredient (Feldman, 2005). The findings seem tenable across cultures, and it is prudent to surmise that marriages fail due to the impact of individualistic belief system.

5

Conceptualizing Love

LIKING

THE PHENOMENON OF LOVE is difficult to be studied and observed scientifically, so that social psychologists have resisted studying this phenomenon for decades. However, because of the importance of love in human interactions, social psychologists have recently started studying this phenomenon. A large body of research on the concept of liking attests to the concept of love. It is therefore crucial to deal with the issue of what makes one person likes another before dealing directly with the construct of love. For decades, social psychologists have conducted research on interpersonal attraction or close relationships. Interpersonal attraction deals with factors that cause the development and sustenance of friendships. Researchers are in agreement with the key variables in interpersonal attraction, such as proximity, physical attractiveness and similarity.

Proximity

Proximity is the most single important factor in understanding the concept of attraction. Geographical location is important because if a person is not in touch with someone, personal attraction will not occur. Proximity is a powerful vehicle as it provides a vital link to geographical distance and how often persons come in contact (Myers, 2005). Proximity is crucial because it facilitates interaction and repeated exposure to a person is potent enough to produce attraction (Feldman, 2005). Proximity allows for anticipated interaction, which has a positive effect on liking and allows for 'familiarity which does not breed contempt' (Myers, 2005; Santrock, 2006).

Physical Attractiveness

There is widespread disagreement on the role of physical attractiveness as one of the key attributes of interpersonal relationships. In the advertising industry, for example, physical attraction has been lauded as the most important factor, but research has not supported this (Santrock, 2006). With gender differences, research has shown that physical attractiveness is more important for a woman than for a man (Myers, 2005, p. 432). Physical attractiveness determines whether or not individuals like each other based on the matching phenomenon: "The tendency for men and women to choose as partners those who are a 'good match' in attractiveness and other traits" (Myers, 2005, p. 433) suggests that a person tends to have as his or her friend or marry someone who is similar in intelligence and attractiveness. However, two persons who are not compatible in physical attractiveness can be happily married because the less attractive person will have qualities that compensate (Myers, 2005). We also have a tendency to equate physical attractiveness with goodness and therefore are more drawn to physically attractive persons.

Attractiveness is dependent on cultural understanding, as well as one's own standards of judgment. Whatever one's culture presents as attractive, one's own understanding of attractiveness will be impacted. Persons who are similar to us tend to be more attractive. Therefore, the more in love a person is, the more attractive he or she finds the loved one and even sees others as less attractive (Myers, 2005). When one is deeply in love with someone there is no easy distraction by the attractiveness of another potential mate because one tends not to pay attention to another person.

Similarity

Myers (2005) views similarity as an important construct in relationships by the maxim 'birds of a feather do flock together' (p. 442). There is no confirmed evidence that opposites do attract but we tend to like persons who are similar to us. The more similar persons are to us, the more we like them. Feldman (2005) states that "one reason similarity increases the likelihood of interpersonal attraction is that we assume that people with similar attitudes will evaluate us positively" (p. 554). Social psychologists believe that similarity breeds content while dissimilarity breeds contempt (Myers, 2005). Balance theory gives credence to the similarity construct because when two persons like each other and agree on a topic there is balance. When there is a disagreement there will be an imbalance, but because they like each other, an attempt will be made to restore balance (Baron and Byrne, 2000).

Reciprocity of liking effect

Social psychologists have confirmed the reciprocity of liking effect, which states that we have the proclivity to like those who like us. If an individual likes another individual the probability that the individual will like him or her in return is high (Feldman, 2005, p. 554). In order for a person to like you in return, he or she has to believe that your motive is pure. Attraction is also affected by one's own self-esteem (Cook and Douglas, 1998). It is also possible to like someone that one had initially disliked (Myers, 2005). Research confirms that this can result in the blossoming of a very strong love relationship. On the other hand, if one ingratiates with a person for the wrong reason it can lead to serious disaster, overwhelming hurt and pain when it is discovered that the person was only behaving nicely to make a good impression.

Cost and benefits

We are attracted to persons based on the cost and benefits of the interaction. A person would be happier to be around a person who allows her or him to feel good about herself or himself yet finds it repulsive when interests are dissimilar. Our own satisfaction and gratification are important factors in the attraction spectrum (Myers, 2005). We like those who reward us and those whom we associate with reward through warmth, trustworthiness, and responsiveness (Myers, 2005). The benefit of being with an attractive person is that others tend to treat a person nicely when the perception is that the individual is attractive. Some persons tend to equate attractiveness with goodness. When we are in close proximity it costs less time and energy to maintain friendship. Individuals are more likely to be affirmed by persons who are similar to them in significant ways which can lead to personal attraction.

The essence of attraction

Studies conducted by anatomist David Berliner (as cited in Goldman, 1994) debunked the view that pheromones affect only animals. There is evidence of human pheromones, which are airborne chemicals that may have a profound impact on us. Pheromones are subconscious forces, which, given the results of research so far, make humans "unwittingly slaves to odorless chemicals, [but] our passion is the result of not just pheromones but poetry, pretty faces . . . and pricey restaurants" (Goldman, 1994, p. 4). McClintock (as cited in Gupta and Lynch, 2002) estimates that pheromones can influence attraction by at least making women "attracted to the smell of a man . . . genetically similar—but not too similar—to their dads" (p. 2).

Impact of the Looking Glass Self

The looking glass self as a concept within the field of sociology has implications for the theory of attraction. The self is viewed as a social product and the looking glass self is a concept that states that we come to see ourselves how others see us. This concept is Symbolic Interaction Theory, the belief that "individuals possess a 'self-concept', or image of themselves, that is built-up, reinforced or modified in the process of interaction with other members of the society" (Haralambos and Holborn, 1995, p. 816). This concept is supported by the self-fulfilling prophecy hypothesis that infers that a belief can fulfill itself on its own. What others believe about us has a way of happening be it negative or positive (Myers, 2005).

The looking glass self simply means that we learn to see ourselves the way that others see us (Yeung and Martin, 2003). People who have authority over us tend to have a profound impact on our self-concept because we are inclined to internalize their views of us and see ourselves as they see us. Yeung and Martin (2003) present clinical data in support of this theory that we adjust our self-concept in line with the views of the person to whom we are attracted or become attracted to persons who see us the way we see ourselves (p. 873). It is also tenable that we adjust our behaviors based on the views of others. Children seem to have an accurate perception of how their parents see them (Cook and Douglas, 1998). Low self-esteem can lead to relationship insecurities because of the looking glass self phenomenon (Murray and Holmes, 2000; Murray, Holmes, McDonald, and Ellsworth, 1998). Symbolic social influence, which states that we can be influenced by the real or imagined presence of someone whom we respect, gives further support to the concept of the looking glass self because we can respect someone so much that we strive to live up to his or her expectations of us and thus see our self the way the person sees us.

Impact of Motivation

The subject of motivation has been given considerable attention for centuries. It has been defined as "the factors that direct and energize the behavior of humans and other organisms" (Feldman, 2005, p. 301). In an attempt to explain motivation, psychologists have put forward a number of approaches, which include the instinct approach, drive reduction approach, arousal approach, incentive approach, cognitive approach, and Maslow's hierarchy (Feldman, 2005). There is intrinsic and extrinsic motivation (Myers, 2005). Regardless of the approach that is considered, what is clear is that motivation has cognitive, biological and social aspects attributed to it (Feldman, 2005). All the approaches elaborated above can help in understanding even the cause of a single instance of motivation.

Plato believed that there are three sources of motivation in people: the drive or desire to satisfy instinct; preservation of sense of self; and the desire for understanding and truth (Waterfield, 1993). Whether one is attracted to a person because of his or her need for relationship, love and belonging, satisfaction of sexual desire, and understanding of the opposite sex more deeply, motivation seems to play a significant role in attraction.

Although our study is not exhaustive, our observations indicate that many factors contribute to liking. In a study among 40,000 participants, Feldman (2005) summarized the results of the research study, which indicated that in descending order, friendship qualities that people value included keeping confidence, loyalty, warmth and affection, supportiveness, frankness, sense of humor, willingness to make time, independence, good conversationalist, and intelligence (p. 544). The ineluctable conclusion is that there are important positive character traits, conduct, communication skills and social skills that affect liking.

LOVE

The love phenomenon has been conceptualized in many ways. Myers (2005) concedes that "loving is more complex than liking and thus more difficult to measure, more perplexing to study" (p. 452). It is very challenging to define and measure love. Researchers initially attempted to distinguish between love and mere liking (Feldman, 2005). Their findings were significant because they recognized that the concept of love is different from liking psychologically. They found that "long-term loving is not merely an intensification of initial liking" (Myers, 2005, p. 452).

Others have postulated that there are basically two main types of love: passionate or romantic love and companionate or affectionate love (Feldman, 2005). Passionate love is seen as the first stage of love. It is "a state of intense longing for union with another" (Myers, 2005, p. 453) or "a state of intense absorption in someone that includes intense physiological arousal, psychological interest, and caring for the needs of another" (Feldman, 2005, p. 555). It involves being sexually aroused by a member of the opposite sex whom someone views as attractive. Companionate love is the second stage and is the result of decreased passion, which allows for the steadying of the relationship. It is "the strong affection we have for those with whom our lives are deeply involved" (Feldman, 2005, p. 555). Companionate love is what deepens the relationship through mutually rewarding and shared experiences (Myers, 2005).

Psychologist Robert Sternberg conceptualized a very detailed explanation of eight kinds of love based on three important components of decision/commitment, intimacy, and passion in his love triangle (Myers, 2005). For Sternberg (as cited in Baron and Byrne, 2000), the kind of love is based on the absence or presence of commitment, intimacy and passion in the relationship. Hassebrauck and Buhl (1996) state that:

> These dimensions are thought to represent the emotional, motivational, and cognitive *components of love* relationships. Each dimension contributes to the quantity *of love* in a relationship. The quality *of* a relationship is represented by the relative magnitude *of* each *component*. (p. 1)

Love is strongest when all three components are present. Non-love has none of the components listed above. Liking has only intimacy; romantic love has intimacy and passion; infatuation has only passion; fatuous love has passion and commitment. Empty love has only decision/commitment; companionate love has intimacy and commitment; and consummate love has intimacy, passion and commitment. Therefore consummate love is the fullest and strongest kind of love (Santrock, 2006).

Lee, Hendricks and Hendricks (as cited in Myers, 2005) also conceptualized several love styles. They theorized that there are three primary love styles which are "eros (self-disclosing passion), ludus (uncommitted game play), and storge (friendship)—which like the primary colors, combine to form secondary love styles" (Myers, 2005, p. 453). Aside from the primary love style, secondary love styles are mania (possessive love), pragma (logical love), and agape (selfless love). Baron and

Byrne (2000) suggest that there are six love styles, which "result in quite different attitudes about interpersonal relationships and quite different behaviors as well" (p. 332).

The wheel theory of love proposed by Reiss (as cited in Turner and Helms, 1995) has four components. The first component is rapport, which has to do with feeling at ease with each other. The second component is self-revelation in the disclosure of personal details about each other's lives. The third component is mutual dependency, developing a reliance on one another and establishing interdependence. The fourth and final component is personality and need fulfillment to satisfy each other's emotional needs. Reiss (as cited in Turner and Helms, 1995) further suggests that, in a serious, long-lasting intimate relationship, the wheel will turn indefinitely; it may turn only a few times in a short-lived romance. Finally, "the weight of each component will cause the wheel to move forward or backward" (Turner and Helms, 1995, p. 450).

From observation there are multifarious models for describing the concept of love. However, none of the models, when examined, seems to be comprehensive. What is clear is that factors, such as mutual understanding, enjoying the loved one's company, giving and receiving support, are indispensable ingredients to all loving relationships (Myers, 2005). The conceptualizations of love, previously described, help us to understand the various types of love with the manifestation of love styles as they relate to relationships. Love is multifaceted and multidimensional, and a complex human experience. The demonstration of love in a relationship, for example, is the interaction between multifarious variables. Other factors within the love construct will be examined by an exposition of other elements in the love phenomenon.

Compassion

Although balance theory accounts for what happens when we don't like the opinion of someone that we love, there is no explanation of what happens when others hurt us deeply. The basic issue then has to do with the factor that is embedded in the intimacy, passion, and commitment when using Sternberg's (as cited in Baron and Byrne, 2000) conceptualization of love as point of reference. The conceptualizations that we have previously examined have not given any explanation for this. Compassion seems to be the first missing link.

The etymology of compassion has Middle English derivations. Its origin can be traced to Anglo-French or Latin and Anglo-French sources. The word comes from the Latin "compassio, from compati to sympathize, from Latin *com-* + *pati* to bear, suffer..." (Compassion, 2008). The prefix "com" means with, together, jointly, or thoroughly (Com-, 2008). The word may be also defined as "sympathetic consciousness of others' distress together with a desire to alleviate it" (Compassion, 2008).

The concept of compassion suggests an understanding of a partner's emotional state and other life problems. Compassion generates generosity, empathy, sympathy and mercy which are at the core of one's understanding of human brokenness and bondage. Compassion puts the need for forgiveness in perspective and encourages compromise and introspection. It facilitates objective reflection and sincere responses and actions to initiate, strengthen or reciprocate human love. A relationship without compassion has no firm foundation. An examination of the concept of forgiveness is crucial in order to see how it relates to compassion.

Forgiveness has positive effect on relationships, even if only in the initial stages according to research findings (Enright and Fitzgibbons, 2000; Fincham, Beach, and Davila, 2004, 2007; Maio, Thomas, Fincham, and Carnelley, 2008; McNulty, 2008). Enright and Fitzgibbons (2000) declare that persons have departed from the moral, philosophical, and religious roots of forgiveness. This seems to be well founded because there is significant difference in how forgiveness is conceptualized among researchers (Mullett, Girard, and Bakhshi, 2004). Enright and Fitzgibbons (2000) clearly demonstrate the importance of forgiveness by examining the roots of forgiveness from the moral, religious, and philosophical perspectives and suggest that:

> Forgiveness is the overarching principle of beneficence with corollary principles of unconditional worth and moral love. Also included in the definition of forgiveness are the moral emotions of compassion and the expression of generosity. All of these qualities, properly understood and practiced, are concerned with human welfare and, therefore, qualify as good." (p. 254)

Enright and Fitzgibbons (2000), in an historical examination of the construct acknowledged that literature from the "Hebrew, Christian, Islamic, Hindu, and Buddhist viewpoints, illustrate that forgiveness occurs within the context of moral right and wrong, and involves reduced resentment and increased compassion and moral love, culminating in transformation" (p. 258). Therefore, forgiveness has to do with a personal responsibility to let go of the hurt and resentment and respond to the offender in a loving way. It involves a move from negative emotion to positive emotions (Mullett, Girard, and Bakhshi, 2004). Forgiveness can be viewed as a metaphor in the forgiveness of God/Yahweh towards His people in the Hebrew and Christian literature which "includes the abandonment of resentment and the application of beneficence" (Enright, and Fitzgibbons, 2000, p. 261).

Forgiveness is a key to the longevity of relationship. Its reality lies in the paradox that those with whom we are deeply in love are the ones who are more prone to hurt us especially in deep intimate relationships. Fincham, Beach, and Davila (2004) state that "spouses report that the capacity to seek and grant forgiveness is one of the most important factors contributing to marital longevity and marital satisfaction" (p. 72). We have seen that forgiveness moves one towards compassion because forgiveness involves the emotion of compassion. Therefore a return to the historical roots of forgiveness is important so that the original connotations and meanings will not become meaningless.

Compassion then sustains the friendly social atmosphere in a relationship in the internalization of knowledge about relationship and prompts an individual to proper action. It has the power to move a person from self-centeredness to other-centeredness. It has the generative power to slow a person down when he or she is forgetting important responsibilities. Compassion is the "brake system" in a relationship. We make withdrawals in our relationships that affect trust without even knowing and therefore we have to stop and seek to understand persons so that we can make deposits to rebuild trust. If one has no brake system, he or she is in serious trouble because human brokenness and bondage necessitate the use of brakes. A lack of compassion therefore weakens commitment to a relationship.

The concept of human brokenness and bondage needs to be clarified and of which there are three prevailing views on human nature. Human beings are viewed as essentially good (the optimistic view) and on the other hand as essentially evil (the pessimistic view). The third view (plasticity) is a combination of the optimism and pessimism viewpoints (Wolfe, 2008). The Judeo-Christian tradition primarily sees human beings as essentially evil, prone to do evil rather than good. Human beings are by nature selfish and hence prone to hurt each other. The need for compassion is underscored by the depravity of human beings and provides an awareness of our struggle between good and bad. We struggle with weaknesses that we yearn to overcome.

The Johari Window of Love

Something that is nominal does not really exist because for something to exist, its constituents must be present (Hasker, 1983). If none of its constituents is present then it does not exist. But do all its constituents have to be present for it to exist? Yes. If components are not present it does not exist. However, all the constituents don't have to be present in totality for something to exist because it does not have to be perfect to be in existence. If we say then that the components of love are intimacy, passion, and commitment, there can be no such thing as non-love because none of the constituents is present. Furthermore, it is not love if all its constituents are not present. If only some of the constituents are present then it is seen to be pseudo. Does there have to be only perfect love for love to exist? Love can exist in degrees of intensity and therefore one can have more or less of it, but it only exists by the presence of its elements.

The conceptualization of love by Sternberg (as cited in Baron and Byrne, 2000) discussed earlier is deficient when the philosophical test of reality is applied due to only consummate love having all the elements. A better model is needed to account for the kinds of love, which takes into consideration all the components of love. It seems useful to propose that this deficiency is the second missing link in the conceptualizations of love.

If we believe that consummate love is the strongest kind of love because it involves intimacy, passion, and commitment, then compassion is the first missing link because love should have four elements instead of three. There needs to be a different kind of love that accounts for the four elements. This kind of love, I believe, should be called authentic love with the components of passion, intimacy, commitment, and compassion. Persons become what I call compassionate-consummate-partners which is a relationship in which an understanding of human brokenness and bondage leads to compassion. Intimacy, passion and commitment will lead to consummate partnership on the other hand. These are the foundations and building blocks of authentic love which incorporates all the components of love in high intensity.

The relational patterns in marriage present four dimensions of love, which can be analyzed on the basis of the degree of intensity of the components of love that are present. Love tends to wear different faces as components present in a relationship. It will determine the kind of love that drives the relationship as illustrated graphically by figure 1 called the Johari Window of Love.

AIMLESS LOVE

Aimless love is low in compassion, commitment, intimacy and passion and exists in form but not essence. This kind of love is associated with mere words and characterized by impressive and expressive vocalization. It is based on blind faith and not the exercise of practice of what one ought to do. In this kind of love, a man and woman come together but remain separated in thought and actions. There is no concept of a union driving their connection with each other therefore the relationship is void of core values which are shared by both partners.

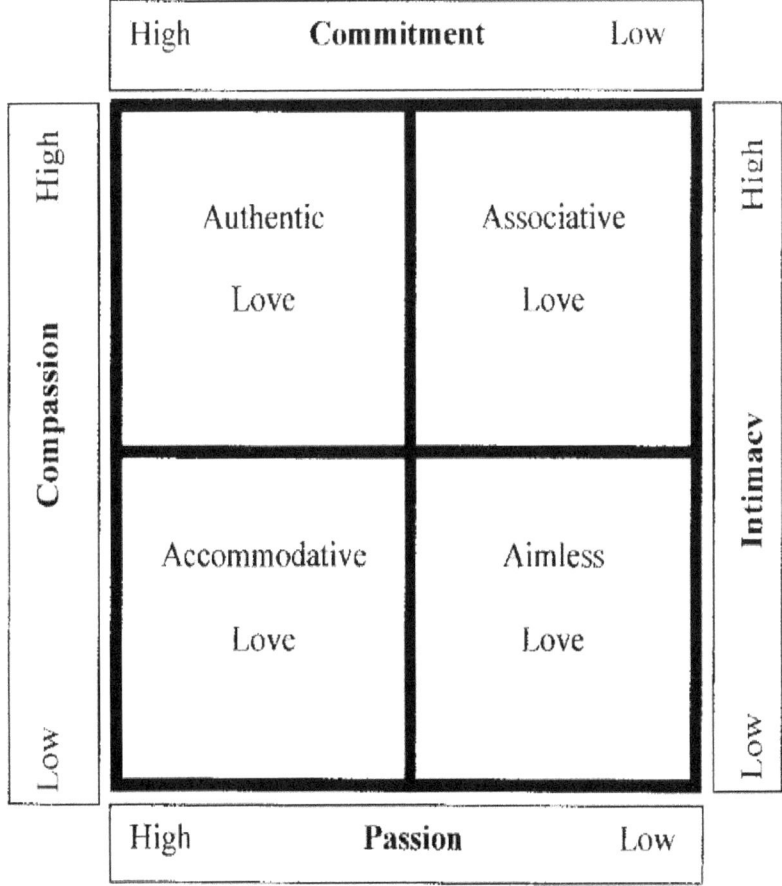

Figure 1: The Johari Window of Love

Some persons are married for years but have difficulty enjoying their relationship. They just go through the motions each day, presenting to the external world a positive picture of their relationship but there is disconnect with the reality that they are experiencing. This is the kind of love that allows for the creation of a special world (adultery) with someone else when one's partner is absent. In this kind of love, flattery is merely ingratiation, serving one's own purpose (Myers, 2005).

Aimless love uses social influence innovations such as the foot-in-the door technique, beginning with a small request then graduating to a bigger request; the door-in-the-face technique, beginning with a bigger request and then move to a smaller when one disagrees and the not-so-free-gift technique, giving a person something that makes him or her feel obligated and finds it hard not to comply with request, as a form of manipulation (Feldman, 2005).

Aimless love is a casual kind of love, which extends mere human courtesies without any significant involvement. It thrives only on external support, living together and sharing space without sharing life. People in this kind of love relationship are mentally, emotionally, psychologically, and spiritually separated and are not intertwined. Their objective is to use each other which then leads to divorce. It is possible for a love life that started out great to deteriorate into aimless love.

Aimless love rejects restrictions and operates only on its own terms and conditions. Persons in this kind of love relationship believe that they must be allowed to do whatever they like without being questioned or have to account for their behaviors. Aimless love is void of being guided by the foundational principles of responsibility and restrictions. In a healthy relationship the terms of the relationship are clearly stated and one is expected to act in the best interest of each other and the relationship which is absent in aimless love.

Aimless love is guided by a philosophy that many vocalize or at least live by without vocalizing. The philosophy that a man must do whatever pleases him is male-oriented. One cannot love his or her partner and continue to do whatever is pleasing only to himself or herself. Aimless love is based on a continuation of the desire to please self amidst one's union with his or her spouse.

Love for one's partner will continue to be aimless until an individual deliberately maintains intimacy, passion, commitment and compassion in the relationship for the empowerment of one's spouse because aimless love has divided loyalty and is self-serving and self-seeking. It is a relationship in which partners are not intentionally caring for the total well-being of each other through the fulfillment of emotional needs.

It is said that the road to success is not a straight line but dotted with many curves. Aimless love turns the curves into circles and it is a love that is dying. This is where persons give up on each other and seek to dissolve their union.

Aimless love is a love that has grown cold and hardened by experiences. In this kind of love, both partners are cold towards each other by rejection and non acceptance and a refusal to forgive. There is selfishness in decision making and a self-centeredness in choices made through a deliberate attempt to stop caring for the total well-being of each other.

Partners who experience this kind of love relationship are hurt, angry and disappointed. They are unwilling to let each other back into their special world and hence determined to protect themselves from each other for fear of being hurt again. These persons feel compelled to build a wall of separation between them. Aimless love is built on a principle that allows love to be reduced to specific conditions and when not met, love will be short-circuited from the heart.

Accommodative Love

Accommodative love is low in compassion and intimacy and high in passion and commitment. Accommodative love is based on a decision to love one's partner regardless of what is happening. There is a strong desire for each other and a resolute commitment to keep one's promise to maintain the relationship. The basis for the continuation of the relationship lies in the fact that one has already made a commitment to maintain passion in the relationship.

Accommodative love is based on a decision to stay in the marriage without a commitment to work on improving it. Difficulties are accommodated instead of working through problems in order to be intimate with each other. There is no compassion or true forgiveness. People stay together because of limited options or because they do not want to negatively affect their children, families or friends by a separation. The experience of intimacy is very low in this kind of love and is even deprived of spiritual connection. There is no understanding of human brokenness and bondage or true forgiveness. Bitterness, anger, malice, unforgiveness and coarse language are characteristics of one's inner life and the interactions with one's partner which causes the relationship to be more susceptible to failure because of a lack of connection at a deeper level. The bitterness and strife involved in the relationship are at the unconscious level as situations force a couple to be more intimate.

In accommodative love persons are prepared to go so far and no more with restrictive boundaries as it relates to how intimate one becomes. There is no deliberate attempt to strengthen the intimacy in the relationship or to work at forgiving from the heart. Forgiveness is only offered at the cognitive level as a way of trying to appease one's self. People keep wishing that they were married to someone else. Individuals with a moral or religious worldview tend to even wish that their partner would die so they could marry someone else. They are accommodative of the relationship but wish it to end soon through the death of their partner.

Compassion and intimacy cannot therefore develop in a relationship that is void of a proper understanding of human brokenness and bondage. The relationship cannot exist when an individual is willing to cling to "unforgiveness," a lack of true readiness to forsake every thought and concept that is damaging to the relationship.

Associative Love

Associative love is low in passion and commitment and high in compassion and intimacy. This kind of love is high in compassion because one seeks to identify with human capacity for sinful acts. Whenever one is treated unfairly it is easily pushed aside because one was expecting it. Persons do not take the time to process their true feelings.

In this kind of love, one readily accepts the excuses for failure on the premise that one is a human being prone to make mistakes. One will hear ladies for instance saying "that is how men are." The positive in this kind of love is that it acknowledges the potential for human beings to make mistakes.

Associative love is high in intimacy and tends to keep the lines of communication open. Issues are dealt with on the basis of "that is how you are but I still love you." The couple continues to share space and life in several ways but still feeling cheated. There is no commitment to the relationship because an individual does not know when the other party might decide to end the relationship.

AUTHENTIC LOVE

Authentic love is high in compassion, commitment, intimacy and passion in contrast to the other types of love, which are high and low (or just low) in some elements of the components of love. Authentic love is very high in all the components of love and there is a true understanding of human brokenness and bondage which patterns the love that God has for humanity. Partners living by this kind of love are committed to each other, compassionate, intimate and passionate. They are committed to caring for the total well-being of each other. It includes genuine soul care; caring for the whole person as a bio-psycho-spiritual care. Authentic love caters to the whole person, body, mind, spirit, and soul which is not an exhaustive list because man or woman is not dichotomous, tripartite or quadripartite but a composite whole.

Authentic love is learning to love to the extent that one is able to love out of the overflow of one's love. It is only a heart of true and full compassion that can love completely. Authentic love, for example, is probably being practiced by many who genuinely love alcoholic partners, abusive partners, and unfaithful partners. This does not imply that one should put herself or himself at risk in abusive situations as noted above. This kind of love is analogous to altruism or prosocial behavior which has to do with "a motive to increase another's welfare without conscious regard for one's self-interests" (Myers, 2005, p. 476). It is not merely social exchange or reciprocity but involves being philanthropic.

Authentic love requires full surrender (Benner, 2003). However, a person will not surrender completely to love easily because of its dualistic nature. Love as a psycho-spiritual experience is both spiritual and mental, leading to a discovery that both comforts and threatens. On one hand, it produces comfort in the sense that one knows that he or she is loved and accepted with strengths and weaknesses. Authentic love causes one to feel a sense of belonging and lessens the reality of loneliness. In contrast, it becomes threatening for an individual who reasons that he or she is not deserving of such great love. One becomes concerned about weaknesses affecting the quality of love being experienced. One will be concerned about whether or not a partner's weaknesses will affect the quality of love as a result of a shared human experience of brokenness and bondage. This threat produces fear, which tends to operate at the unconscious level, hence crippling one's ability to surrender to love.

Love cannot thrive where there is fear and only perfect love can drive out all fear.

In surrendering to love, one can anticipate becoming vulnerable due to demands for self-disclosure (Myers, 2005). There is no genuine love without vulnerability. Love is a pulley-wheel, it can bear more than one can ever imagine if it is properly balanced and made up of the right material. One should develop authentic love and the marital skills to sustain it. A spouse's love will become authentic with a decision to love in the same manner when comparing one's love to that of a Supreme Supernatural Being.

If one is prepared to die for her or his partner then one must also be willing to go the distance to care for her or him and work to resolve any conflict in the relationship. One should not merely seek to make choices to love one's partner but choose to love her or him. When an individual chooses to love her or his partner, the choices made on a daily basis will be geared at confirming one's decision. A person does not have the full capacity to love authentically if he or she is not a whole person because being a whole person is a prerequisite for authentic love. In order to be a whole person, one needs to be healed and liberated in every area, including physical, spiritual, psychological, emotional, mental and social.

In order to love one's partner authentically one has to desire one's partner just for who he or she is. This means that a person will love on a personal decision. If one makes a willful decision one is just operating in one's own personal power. It is one's willingness not one's willfulness that will enable the expression of love authentically (Benner, 2005).

Authentic love protects against invasion, intrusion, and infiltration (which is the most deadly because it includes a heart attitude of willfulness to hold on to or create destructive contemplation and carryout destructive acts, instead of willingness to love out of a mature personhood). When a spouse protects the private little kingdom of marriage, there will be a relationship that is secure, stable and serene. This is the basis of authentic love.

Authentic love requires action not just feeling, for example, in keeping love alive. If love requires expression, it is an art that can be learned. A couple can learn to love better by looking out for the best interests of each other due to a high regard and esteem of each other. Authentic love is a unique kind of love which models God's love as it teaches us how to express and experience holistic love. The love that a spouse has for his or her partner must become a replica of the love that God has for humanity and the love that one should have for God. One's love for his or her spouse should promote the overall well-being within the marriage which is actually the overall well-being of one's self. One should strive to treat his or her spouse with favor.

Authentic love leads to secure attachment which is being connected without being enmeshed. Authentic love leads to trust; knowing that one can confide in one's partner without reservation because one knows that his or her partner does not renege on his or her promises. Authentic love leads to caring; feeling compelled to do just about anything for one's partner. It suggests that couples' lives must become intertwined without being enmeshed. It fosters a relationship built and sustained on trust, tolerance of flaws and idiosyncrasies, empowerment, care and warmth. This kind of attitude empowers a person to do things to keep compassion alive, maintain intimacy, keep the passion going, and strengthen the commitment.

Authentic love seems to explain the deeper dimensions of love in contrast to the other reviewed conceptualizations. It demonstrates that one continues to love one's partner not because she or he is perfect but due to a shared human struggle and an ability to sympathize. Love is a moral virtue and one demonstrates that she or he possesses this virtue by doing good and practicing behaviors that are loving behaviors as one strives to maintain balance and consistency of love in the relationship.

6

The Historicity of Human Sexuality

THE SCIENTIFIC HISTORY OF human sexuality is fairly recent. John B. Watson was "'one of the first Americans to investigate the physiological aspects of adult human sexual responses'" (Magoun, 1981, p. 369) which makes him one of the foremost experimental psychologists to research adult human sexual behavior, with the study of questionnaires based on films on sex hygiene after World War I. The emphasis on sex prompted Watson to investigate human behavior in more detail (Magoun, 1981). Watson studied the attitudes of doctors towards sex and sex education as a means to mitigate the spread of venereal diseases. The attitude of some doctors in the nineteenth century was so moralistic that sex is viewed as a kind of disease. Watson became convinced that the study of sex could not be left up to the medical professionals so psychologists needed to study sex directly (Magoun, 1981). Watson did extensive research, and it is believed that he connected his own body and that of his female partner to instruments that he developed, while making love and thus produced probably the first reliable data on human sexual responses. His research strategies seemed to have negatively affected his career (Magoun, 1981).

Others, however, have rejected the claim that Watson actually conducted this laboratory study, dismissing it as gossip. Benjamin, Whitaker, Ramsey, and Zeve (2007) claim that "the evidences for and against the research allegedly conducted by Watson are insufficient and that the story of the sexual study is a gossip" (p. 131). Notwithstanding the difficulty inherent in ascertaining that Watson did laboratory work on human sexuality, it is without doubt that he sparked and fostered research in this area.

Havelock's 1905 contribution to the sexual research debate consisted of a detailed and patient evaluation, consisting of information contained in case histories, in an effort to separate fact from fiction (Neiger, 1966, p. 103). From this perspective, the progress continued with Dickinson (Neiger, 1966), who built on the foundation of Havelock Ellis in 1931 and 1933 when he furthered "knowledge by combining basic science training with keen clinical observation" (Neiger, 1966, p. 103). The work of Ford and Beach in 1951 "provided extremely significant detailed observations of the physiological, psychological and social factors in the sexual behavior of animals and man" (Neiger, 1966, p. 103).

In 1921, a Bureau of Social Hygiene was established in New York City, with financial support by Rockefeller, a philanthropist, to promote a substantial program of research involving problems of sex (Magoun, 1981, p. 373). In 1929, a publication called Research on Marriage reported details of the sexual behaviors of one hundred females and males (Magoun, 1981). Based on the historical records, the study of sex was always met with resistance, demonstrated by the work of Kinsey. In 1973, Kinsey reluctantly decided to give a course on sex education and marriage to students at Indiana University. He found little information in its library on the subject. He decided to teach the facts, so he had to do the research. Kinsey developed interviewing techniques geared to gather an appropriate sex history, and by the end of the first year he reportedly collected 300 sexual histories (Pomeroy as cited in Magoun, 1981, p. 375). The findings were met with resistance from those who believed that the work was disgraceful to academic pursuit and rallied to have him dismissed from the university because of his radical ideas.

Reiss (cited in Neiger, 1966) wrote a lot about the changing attitudes in the United States in the 1960s. His research consisted of using questions on background history with a twelve item Guttman Scale on premarital sexual permissiveness. Reiss (cited in Neiger, 1966) was able to obtain reliable results on sexual permissiveness. Neiger (1966) reports that a lot of the findings were very interesting as observed, for example, in the similarity of social class and permissiveness. Neiger (1966) further notes the characteristic weakness of early work done on this area was that of methodology, as researchers relied heavily on case histories and these empirical studies were all prone to error based on the indirect method of reporting on past behavior. Reiss (cited in Neiger, 1966) determined that there was a need to establish these findings more objectively through direct observations in order to decrease errors based on the indirect method of reporting. Credit is therefore given to Harlow, who, in 1965, through his study with rhesus monkeys, helped to establish the fact that learning is a prerequisite for sexual response (Neiger, 1966).

Masters and Johnson (1961) carried out laboratory work without Professor Kinsey's knowledge in 1961 and 1966 that contributed to the 1960s established scientific facts related to sexual behavior. The work of Masters and Johnson on human sexuality has been lauded by the academic community (McCarthy, 1973; Neiger, 1966; Bruni, 1974). Masters and Johnson's seminal study was groundbreaking although it raised some ethical concerns relating to methodology as they directly observed and made color movies of external and internal events in males and females during masturbation, artificial and natural coition. From this laboratory study, the researchers came up with the classic model of the human sexual response. Basson (2000) agrees that one of the interpretations of Masters and Johnson's sexual work is "the traditional model for the human sex response cycle . . . represented as Desire → arousal → orgasm → resolution (Kaplan, 1979; Masters and Johnson, 1966)" (p. 53). In contrast, the female sexual response cycle of Masters and Johnson, as interpreted by Neiger (1966), presents an alternative viewpoint giving the four phases of sexual response as 1) initial excitement phase; 2) plateau phase; 3) orgasmic phase; 4) resolution phase. However, there is no significant disparity in the two interpretations between the terms "desire and initial excitement."

Basson (2000) argues that the male sexual response is more easily understood than the more controversial female response. Basson (2000) concedes that Masters and Johnson's study has been relatively useful for understanding men's sexual function and dysfunction as well as establishing some key facts about sexuality in male and female. However, regarding key facts about sexuality in male and female, research has confirmed that "in the human female, sexual activity is generally not confined to any period of heat, although some studies indicate an increase at about the time of ovulation. Others show some increase near the menses" (Ganong, 1973, p. 179). It is also established that "ovariectomy does not necessarily reduce libido . . . or sexual ability" (Ganong, 1973, p. 175) and that men's sexual response is controlled more by testosterones or androgen and that "treatment with sex hormones increases sexual interest and drive in humans" (Ganong, 1973, p. 175).

Neiger's (1966) précis of Masters and Johnson is useful at this point because their study is the only classic study that is available on human sexual response and though his summary is concise it is thorough, by the following illustration:

1. The excitement phase varies from a few minutes to several hours. Vaginal lubrication begins within the first ten to twenty seconds of effective stimulation and is followed by increases in the size of the breast, clitoris, major and minor labia.

2. The plateau phase is a relatively short period, during which the clitoris may retract some fifty percent in over-all length, the inner two-thirds of the vagina expands greatly, while its outer third becomes markedly constricted, forming a so-called orgasmic platform. A vasomotor rash or "sexual flush" occurs in the majority of women, covering the breasts and other parts of the body. This skin reaction corresponds with a marked change in the coloration in the minor labia, which turn cardinal or burgundy red. Once this colour change has occurred, orgasm is impending and inevitable in about 60–90 seconds, provided that stimulation is continued.

3. The orgasmic phase itself lasts three to eight seconds. It involves between four and ten rhythmic contractions of the orgasmic platform, depending on the experienced intensity of the orgasm. In addition, generalized muscular contraction patterns occur not only among the muscle groups of the pelvis and lower abdomen but throughout the body. "The corded neck muscles, the swollen, flushed face and the expanded rib cage are familiar aspects of total female response to sexual tension. (Masters and Johnson, 1961, p. 793).

4. The resolution phase is characterized by a generalized detumescence and return to normal coloration. Normally, this phase lasts 5–15 minutes from the last orgasm, but in women who have reached the plateau phase without being able to proceed to orgasm, it may last hours. This prolonged vasocongestion may be perceived as distinct pelvic discomfort by the woman. (pp. 107–108)

Based on a review of the sexual research literature, Neiger (1966) concludes that the richness of the sexual studies on the female sexual response has resulted in the following observations: 1) there is no difference between clitoral and vaginal stimulation in producing orgasm. The clitoris and vagina go through the same process whether or not the clitoris is directly stimulated; 2) the clitoris gets a lot of stimulation through the traction of the clitoral hood during intercourse and many women do not like continuous direct stimulation of the clitoris, they prefer for the areas around the clitoris to be stimulated; and 3) it is possible for women to have multiple orgasms if stimulation continues before the resolution phase kicks in. These observations suggest that our understanding of human sexual behavior has been significantly affected by Masters and Johnson's study.

Though most sexuality researchers lauded the historical work of Masters and Johnson, Basson (2000) appears to struggle with the application of Masters and Johnson's model to females in some situations. Basson (2000) argues against the research methodology of Masters and Johnson, utilizing volunteers with "normal" sexual response as the control study platform. Basson (2001) proposes that "in order to understand sexual problems, we need to expand concepts of the human sexual response cycle (Bancroft, 1989; Basson, 2000a; Pfaus, 1999; Stayton, 1989; Tiefer, 1991) or employ a number of potentially blended models." (p.33). Basson (2001) believes that Masters and Johnson's model is deficient for the following reasons:

> Four fundamental aspects of women's sexuality health underlie the need for a different model. First, compared to men whose responses are influenced more by testosterone (Bancroft, 1989), women have a lower biological urge to be sexual for release of sexual tension. Second, women's motivation (or willingness) to have sexual experience stems from a number of "rewards" or "gains" that are not strictly sexual, these rewards being additional to, and often is of far more relevance than, the women's biological neediness or urge. These rewards are not irrelevant to men but may be less often the major motivational force. To some degree, men experience their desire as independent of context—often choosing to use the word "drive." Third, women's sexual arousal is a subjective mental excitement that may or may not be accompanied by awareness of vasocongestive changes in her genitalia and other physical nongenital manifestations of arousal. If there is genital awareness, it may or may not be an erotic stimulus to the woman. Fourth, orgasmic release of sexual tension may or may not occur; when it does, it can happen in a variety of ways, even in the one woman. (pp. 52-53)

A critical analysis of the sexuality literature finding underscores the fact that arousal is not subject to romance in either of the sexes on one hand; but, on the other hand, it has failed to demonstrate what happens in a long standing relationship. This observation is potent because when we are accustomed to things they do not necessarily have the same impact on us.

Basson (2001) conducted studies with 47 women with low sexual desire. The results reveal that psychological, emotional factors, situational context, and depression affect the women's desire in various ways. Psychological factors were the most statistically significant for diminishing arousability in 85 percent of the women. The research findings suggest that women's sexual response does not always start with desire as previously proposed by Masters and Johnson. A plausible explanation is that desire could be inhibited by arousability and desire could change due to the length of a relationship.

Gonzaga et al. (2006) contend, as a result of their research, that romantic love and sexual desire should be considered as emotions. The considerations seemed plausible for the proposal of an elaborated cycle to complement Masters and Johnson's classic cycle. Basson (2001) presents an alternative model of human sexual response cycle as a sequential process involving sexual neutrality, sexual stimuli (psychological or biological influences), sexual arousal, sexual desire and arousal, emotional and physical satisfaction, and emotional intimacy. Basson's (2001) cycle seems practical for understanding the female sexual response within a socio-cultural framework. With this model, the female sexual response begins with sexual neutrality and the willingness to experience arousal. Subsequent desire stems from a wish to increase emotional intimacy with a partner. This alternate female sexual response cycle gives credence to the fact that nonsexual issues will affect sexual interest. For example, if a female values complete privacy, she can have a problem responding by the mere unconscious thought that someone might be hearing her responding sexually. It also illustrates that sexual intercourse may be engaged on the basis of increasing emotional intimacy and not on the basis of a need for sexual release.

It is without doubt that Masters and Johnson's classic study on human sexuality is relevant in understanding current trends in human sexuality. However, it is possible for a woman to be diagnosed with a sexual response disorder due to variables in the relationship. Caution needs to be exercised when diagnosing sexual disorders on the part of mental health practitioners and sexologists. Further analysis of Masters and Johnson's classic study needs to be done because it is possible that the study was negatively impacted by our patriarchal legacy. For example, the dominant role of males in the sex act and what females believe about their role due to how they have been treated by males.

There are other factors that affect sexual response and satisfaction. It is worth noting that assumed agreement (the belief that there is unity on critical issues) is associated with marital satisfaction (Levinger and Breedlove, 1960). Therefore, agreement in the relationship is also associated with sexual satisfaction. In addition, although this may be the result of cultural factors, Beck, Bozman and Qualtrough (1991) conclude that "overall, females reported less frequent desire, relative to males" (p. 453). It is reported in The Economist (1994) that men think more about sex than women. Research conducted in the United States indicates that frequency of sex decreases with age (Marriage Partnership, 1995). The result for men confirmed the average number of times per year among different age groups as illustrated in figure 2.

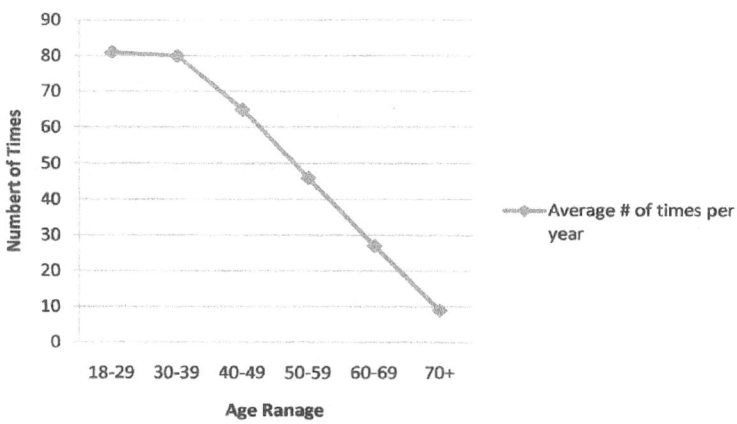

Figure 2

Analysis of 2156 men and 1955 women revealed that couples in their mid-sixties have sex 1.7 times per month (DeLamater, Hyde, and Fong, 2008). This finding is corroborated by Kita's (1998) report from investigation that, according to the University of Chicago's General Social Survey:

> Men have the most sexual intercourse between the ages of 18 and 29. The majority of men in this age-group report bumping bones one or two times a week. After that, the slow, inexorable slide begins. By age 70 . . . [one] can expect to be getting lucky only once a month" (p. 130).

As it relates to sexual satisfaction, Perlman and Abramson (1982) conclude that there are no gender differences in how sexual satisfaction is assessed. Sexual satisfaction is not synonymous with frequency of sexual intercourse as well as intrapsychic variables which are also related to sexual satisfaction. Research confirms that:

> The frequency of sex was correlated with sexual satisfaction. The greater the frequency of orgasm, orgasm with partner, and orgasm during intercourse, the higher the ratings of sexual satisfaction. However, the single most important correlate of sexual satisfaction . . . is how pleasurable sex is evaluated. Other important variables for sexual satisfaction include marital happiness . . . and the absence of sexual anxiety . . . (Perlman and Abramson, 1982, p. 459)

Although this research was carried out in the early eighties, current findings based on our analysis so far support the claim that sexual satisfaction is important in a marital relationship. It is therefore congruent to conclude that sexual satisfaction contributes to marital happiness and marital happiness contributes to sexual satisfaction. It is important to be aware of the frequency rate of sexual intercourse with age and how to enhance the orgasmic experience of both partners.

The issue of sex positions needs to be looked at. It is said that Kama Sutra, which is over 3,000 years old, has a content that has materials geared at making an Indian male able to bring his partner to orgasm from the many ways suggested and thus he should feel extremely inadequate if he is not able to do so (Neiger, 1966). Talmey (1933, 1938) concluded that there are six positions of copulation which have been used by different ethnic races across several epochs. He indicated that these positions are standing, sitting, side by side, man above, man below and from behind. The position most favored for those of us in the Western world is the man above position. It is recognized that:

> In this position the vagina and the erect penis are extended in the same direction and the rubbing of the clitoris against the penis, which are the most sensitive organs for inducing libido, are facilitated. The supine position is mechanically the most favorable for the friction of the most sensitive parts. (Talmey, 1933, 1938, p. 441)

However, based on the study of Masters and Johnson, there does not have to be direct stimulation of the clitoris for the female to experience orgasm. In light of this, couples should feel free to explore and use what works for them at various points.

7

Conceptualizing Marriage

CONCEPTUALIZING MARRIAGE AS A UNION

Our understanding of marriage seems to be bankrupt; we tend to use the wrong formula in attempting to understand it. In reference to the Creation story in the Judeo-Christian Bible previously mentioned, the second account in Genesis chapter 2 records that the Creator said the two shall become one flesh. Jewett (1975) gives a potent analysis of this in affirming that:

> When two people become one flesh, this does not mean that the identity of the one (the wife) [which is normally the view in a biblical patriarchal interpretation] is absorbed into some mystical oneness with the other (the husband), but that both are conformed to a common personality, as it were, of which each partakes, in which each shares, by virtue of the marriage relationship. The common experience of marriage, to the degree that the ideal of oneness is achieved, shapes both partners so that they are congruous to each other [the view that must be taken in an egalitarian marriage, my emphasis!]. (p.140)

Conceding to this kind of understanding, it is tenable to see the formula as more mathematical reasoning than semantic analysis. The two shall become one speaks to product, not sum. In multiplication $1 \times 1 = 1$, but in addition $1+1=2$, this seems to be the difference that needs to be borne in mind. The product is what God makes of us in marriage; the sum is what we continue to think about that perpetuates self-centeredness. In marriage you are the product of your union not the sum of it.

Man and woman are created equal. They are in fellowship and are made complete in their relatedness and equality with each other. Man or woman is not superior to each other; but equal in humanness. In marriage, they are aware of their difference but their focus is on perfecting their oneness. It is a mutual love of unique quality that maintains this oneness (Jewett, 1975, p. 140). Therefore, marriage does not make any inferior or superior but propagates human equality even in oneness.

Some persons with a sum analysis principle speak about the other half or the better half. They argue that ½ + ½ = 1, thus you are the sum of your union. The problem is that the Creator of marriage did not say the two halves shall become one; but the two shall become one. The product principle seems to fit well because ½ × ½ = ¼. Sum thinking keeps us separated but product thinking keeps us intertwined without causing psychological enmeshment. After all, the aim of marriage is for two whole individuals to come together to form a complete union. There will be deficiencies in a marriage with each partner bringing only half of her or him into the relationship.

Arthur (2000) observes that the account of marriage in Genesis speaks to man's responsibility to care for the woman and man's identification with woman. This identity speaks to them becoming one flesh. She further observes that "the identification is so intrinsic and real that when a man loves his wife, he is actually loving himself" (p. 41) and when a woman loves her husband she is actually loving herself. Wallerstein (1994) puts forward that when happily married couples speak about their marriage they speak about what is good for them and what is good for their marriage. He also noticed that when one partner directly does something, the other partner is also credited for it so that both partners are credited for what one partner directly does.

In marriage, a special joining or uniting takes place as the husband and wife engage in sexual intercourse, they become one flesh. They are inseparably joined together. What this means is that if one tries to separate them, one will no longer get two but halves or pieces (Arthur, 2000). This further strengthens the product concept because when one divides the product of 1×1 (1) by two one will get a ½. A couple cannot separate from each other without negatively affecting each other. It is difficult to become two "complete" persons again. Remember that divorce is a paradox; it can cause both pain and pleasure.

One might ask, how do individual differences and personalities fit into this formula? Jewett (1975) notes that creation ordinance suggests that man and woman are properly related when they learn to accept each other as equals with differences that are mutually complementary in all spheres of life and human endeavor (p. 14). Men and women need to accomplish two important tasks before they can be properly related by accepting that they are equal and different but complementary.

Humanity or human beings must be viewed as male and female, as the equality of the sexes composes humanity. Humanity cannot be properly understood if humanity is not seen as male and female in equality and relatedness to each other in fellowship. If marriage is the coming together of a male and female in closer relationship then a deeper fellowship with each other must be based on a separate equality into joint equality. Marriage then could be seen as a kind of joint humanity.

If one uses the reality test of determining existence by using the theory of constituents, then in order for marriage to exist, the components of it must be present. If marriage is made up of male and female in order for marriage to be present, then both male and female species must be present. It is also possible to talk about a strong marriage and a weak marriage depending on the amount of each constituent that is present. One might be tempted to wonder if male and female can be present to a lesser or higher degree. This is a resounding yes; humanity is not just body but a composite of many parts, including the psychological and the emotional. Equality of the sexes in every respect will allow for the strongest marriage which is the ideal oneness to which we are aspirants (Jewett, 1975).

Wallerstein (1994) posits two important tasks that are crucial components of product thinking. The first task is to cognitively separate from the family of origin. This separation seems more difficult for women than men because women seem to be socialized to be more family oriented than men. In the Caribbean, for example, there are many matriarchal single parent families and it is a taboo to be called "mama's boy." The second task of building the marital identity appears to be more crucial. This has to do with "creating the psychological identity of the marriage as an overarching presence, a new corporate identity, representing a "we-ness" in place of two separate "I's," which is deemed a crucial task of early marriage" (Wallerstein, 1994, p. 645). The marital identity in product thinking goes deeper than "we-ness" because it refers to sameness while still recognizing difference. It is a shared identity that results in a new identity seen as a union or a single entity. Product thinking keeps togetherness in place and holds autonomy in balance. In product thinking, togetherness is never sacrificed on the altar of autonomy.

Wallerstein (1994) affirms that if marriage is going to be gratifying and endure, the couple must deal effectively with nine psychological tasks during the early stage of marriage and again at critical periods in the marriage. Wallerstein (1996) sees these nine psychological tasks as 1) consolidating separation and establishing new connection, 2) building the marital identity - togetherness versus autonomy, 3) establishing the sexual life, 4) expanding the marital relationship by making psychological room for children, while still protecting the private sphere of the couple, 5) establishing the marriage as a safe and nurturing zone, 6) building a fun filled and interesting relationship, 7) confronting and mastering the challenges of life while maintaining the strength of the marital bond, 8) providing nurturance and comfort to each other, and 9) keeping the early romantic, idealised images of falling in love alive while dealing with sobering realities. These findings reveal that if the psychological tasks are not properly performed, problems may develop in the marriage sooner or later.

Based on Wallerstein's (1996) psychological tasks, marriage is a complex institution that may even alter the personalities of the partners as a function of balancing for marital success. Studies conducted by Bentler and Newcomb (1978) revealed that personality similarity is important for marital success but correlation similarity does not mean equality in trait level. This gives credence to the fact that personality might be modified to create balance. Bentler and Newcomb (1978) concluded that:

> The interaction of two people in that unique intimate and intense situation called marriage is an immensely complicated process that draws on many factors of each member's background and personality, as well as more situational characteristics. A marriage is the result of what each partner brings to the marriage and what they make of it [allowing their personalities to be altered to create balance], once together. (p. 1069)

Marriage should affect a person's total life. When anything enters one's blood, it flows through the whole body; in like manner, a union affects one's whole life. A spouse cannot leave her or his partner out of any area of her or his life. Intimacy should become ubiquitous in a marriage where one's partner is part of one's total existence. If one spouse is not happy, the other is not happy; whenever a part of a person is experiencing pain the whole body is affected. A person will not be fulfilled if part of him or her is making progress and the other part is not. One's life must be balanced; every part of a person must be given the appropriate attention. One's partner is part of him or her; one should give him or her appropriate attention. If one's partner is not succeeding, one is not completely succeeding. A spouse cannot succeed in isolation of his or her partner.

Product thinking is different from sum thinking, in that sum thinking sees one's partner as adding to him or her. Product thinking sees one's partner as part of his or her whole not an addition to him or her. Product thinking views a couple as so intertwined, that the process of becoming one is lost in the product of being one. When the baker puts various ingredients together to make something, it is no longer referred to in terms of the various ingredients, but the name given to the final product. Marriage is the name given to the final product of a marital union. To use a concept from Gestalt Psychology, one's whole is greater than the sum of one's parts.

Emotional attachment is so pronounced in marriage that when a union is broken, it delivers from pain as well as causes pain. It has also been recognized that when persons have lost their "partner", they experience a kind of loss that is tantamount to literally losing a part of themselves. This feeling is generated because one feels "at one" with his or her partner and when union is broken, it has a ripping and rippling effect on one's life.

Our socialization does not facilitate product thinking. Listen to the way that we make reference to our spouse, "my wife and I or my husband and I." A new paradigm for making reference to one's spouse that facilitates product thinking needs to be advanced, the "I inclusive" paradigm. In this approach, one would say I inclusive (David and Amoy) am very grateful for this opportunity to share with this gathering . . . A covariant of this is, "a part of me (Amoy) was not able to make it to this function."

Could it be that product thinking is at work in marriage at the subconscious level in a negative way when one doesn't take "care" of his or her spouse? It is a tendency for persons to neglect themselves. It is a human tendency to neglect that which is closest; it can be done another time seems to become the predominant mental attitude. How one neglects one's self will result into neglect of his or her partner because the partner is part of him or her. A marriage partner needs to work against this unconscious product thinking and start taking care of himself or herself (I inclusive). This is important because it is extremely challenging to have a meaningful and fulfilling healthy relationship if one is not taking care of himself or herself (Jordan et al., 1999). Self-care ensures that there is partner care.

Product thinking allows a person to take full responsibility for his or her relationship by choosing to impact one's self negatively or positively. As a result of the union, what one does will have an impact on one's marital partner. Change in one part can bring about change in another part. For example, the same way that one takes medication to deal with problems in his or her body, if one gets the right treatment when one's relationship is experiencing problems it can impact the problem positively.

Product thinking will make it possible for a person to save his or her marriage when dealing with himself or herself as he or she is also dealing with his or her partner that is a part of himself or herself. This suggests that one can't deal with one's self without dealing with one's partner. When an individual cheats, one's partner is also experiencing the cheating. If a person is unfair then the other partner is also experiencing the unfairness. When one succeeds or fails one's partner is also experiencing the success or failure and should a divorce occur then the individual is also divorcing himself or herself. When one loves, one's partner experiences love, which also affects the love of the one receiving the love for the one giving the love.

Wheat (1983) echoes this concept in similar terms when he states "you become loveable by loving, not by straining to attract love" (p. 18). One might be wondering how far the author will take this, until one understands that product thinking will change his or her attitude. However, facts alone will not do it as one will need to internalize it and to allow it to change one's attitude by impacting thinking, feelings and actions.

The sociology of learned behavior makes it difficult to change our way of thinking. A spouse probably has been doing things in marriage based on how he or she was taught or what he or she observed (more things are caught than taught) growing up, given the patriarchal legacy. One needs to take the time to learn from those who have studied marriage. One cannot allow one's self to be trapped by an old paradigm when one needs a new paradigm. I am proposing that the sum paradigm is bankrupt due to the impact of the information age on the socio-cultural changes, which would necessitate a product paradigm. The sum paradigm is guided by a patriarchal mindset, while the product paradigm is guided by egalitarianism.

CONCEPTUALIZING MARRIAGE METAPHORICALLY

Metaphors can be very potent in teaching nuggets of truth and can be used to conceptualize marriage. These metaphors of marriage are geared at helping to understand important marital principles. Metaphors are extremely useful in painting pictures of reality and so are important in developing product thinking.

Marriage is a garden that is beautiful when maintained. If one wants his or her garden to remain beautiful, one has to maintain it. In a garden, there are real roses and real thorns and in taking care of the roses, one has to be careful not to damage the rose or be damaged by the thorns. Too much water, fertilizer, sunlight and weeds can ruin the marital garden. There needs to be balance to ensure just enough of what is needed and care taken to remove what is not needed. The paradox is that both what is needed and what is not, can harm the plant. A garden has seasons that must be understood in order to provide the best care of the contents. In comparison to the garden, a spouse should know the season that his or her marriage is going through so that he or she can act in the best interest to preserve the relationship.

Marriage is compared to a motor vehicle that needs regular inspection and servicing to keep functioning properly. There are some areas of the servicing that need expert attention. A spouse needs to know when his or her marriage needs "expert" attention. One cannot keep putting off the warning signals or the vehicle will malfunction. A driver needs to be familiar with the warning signals on his or her vehicle. This translates into the marital relationship where a spouse needs to know his or her partner.

A vehicle that needs fixing will continue to get worse if it is not repaired in a timely manner. One's marriage will get worse if one does not heed the warning signals to deal with the breakdown in the marital relationship. The longer one takes to service one's vehicle when it needs servicing, the more it will potentially cost for servicing. In other words, the longer one takes to "fix" one's marriage the more it will cost in terms of pain and resources. If one doesn't make the sacrifice to fix one's vehicle it will leave him or her on the street. If one doesn't do something about the warning signals in one's marriage, one may lose it.

Marriage is like a seesaw in which to work well adjustments have to be made on both sides to ensure smooth functioning. There has to be balance for the seesaw to work well. Marriage has to manage conflict well in order to survive.

The process of marriage can be compared to a checking account without an overdraft facility. In order for the account to keep current, checks that are drawn must be balanced against funds in the account. If one keeps writing checks without balancing the book, and adding funds to the account, the check will not be cleared. The parallel is, one cannot take out of her or his marriage without putting in effort as it will be found wanting.

Marriage is like water which is considered very necessary for survival. Water has to be controlled in order to serve a good purpose. Water, if it is not controlled can be destructive. It is a powerful source of energy; although it can save or take life. The paradox is that that which is good for a person can also kill him or her if it is not properly handled. An individual needs to treat his or her marriage in such a way that it works effectively, not against him or her. When a person is in the river swimming, the person doesn't fight the current; the person works with the current. In other words, don't fight marriage, work with it.

Marriage is a saw which in order to work well, it has to be properly maintained. Sometimes the saw will accidentally hit something that blunts the edge (teeth). Steps have to be taken for it to continue to work well. Marriage needs to be fixed like the metaphor of the saw, when something goes wrong in order for it to continue to work well. When using the saw, one needs to ensure that he or she is very careful so that he or she doesn't hit things carelessly and frequently. If one is careless, he or she will have to sharpen and set the saw frequently. When this happens, one's productive time is lessened and the saw will "sharpen-out." Marriage has to last a lifetime, be careful with it so that it can last a lifetime.

Marriage is a banyan tree that has aerial prop roots. The aerial prop roots come down and eventually form thick woody trunks which can become indistinguishable from the original trunk and can even cover a large area of land. As a tree gets stronger with age so marriage should get stronger with age. A banyan tree is able to cover a large acreage of land, which makes it very resilient. When it is allowed to grow, it will be able to stand hard times. If one facilitates the growth of his or her marriage, it will be able to stand up to the challenges of life. My first encounter with a banyan tree was impressionable as I admired the beauty of the tree and the way it was able to withstand hurricanes. I was also impressed by the lifespan of the tree and its self-preserving nature. It grows new roots as the years go by. Marriage compared to the longevity and resilience of the banyan tree has the power to succeed if it is allowed to work as it was intended.

Marriage is a magnet and when two magnets share the same environment in close proximity to each other, one of two things happens. They will either repel or connect with each other. In comparison to a magnet, it is important for one to give off the positive although one has the potential for negativity. A person will connect with one's partner and not repel him or her. One should be affable and have a winsome personality and to ensure that the marriage partner is properly positioned to be close without isolating the other individual. The magnet that is free will move to the magnet that is stationary. In other words, a spouse can impact his or her partner positively even when one's partner does not want to do anything. When one is free, initiation of positive contact with his or her partner will ensure irresistibility. A couple should have ardor for each other that will make it impossible for any of them to be distracted or unfaithful in any way.

Marriage is like a marathon which conjures up an image of stamina acquired through intense and careful preparation. In order to succeed at running a marathon, one has to take the time to prepare before entering the race. It requires physical, emotional, psychological, and even spiritual preparation. While in the race, one has to have a general perspective on the distance that he or she has to run. Success will be determined by how well one runs each mile. If one focuses on the number of miles ahead, one might become overwhelmed, but if one takes it one mile at a time one will remain motivated.

The length of the marathon suggests that as conditions change an individual has to learn to adapt to the weather changes. In order to run well, one has to leave unnecessary baggage by developing good strategies during preparation. Many persons have learned the hard way in trying to run a race without adequate preparation as well as effective and efficient strategies.

Marriage is teamwork. Teamwork suggests the same objective of empowering spouses to listen to each other due to the same objective of success in the marriage. Teamwork also implies that there are some procedures to follow and to work with as a team. A couple needs to learn to work as a team. A couple learns to work as a team as they learn to trust each other. Teamwork means that one speaks positively and is free to share one's perspective without feeling intimidation. Watson and Davidson (2006) reported on the finding of Lewis (as cited in Curran, 1983) that healthy marriages tend to have equality between spouses (p. 50). There is no place for intimidation in healthy marriages as equality provides the context for effective communication and teamwork. Farrar (1990) summarizes the effective marital model:

> Gentlemen, your wife is a strategic gift to you! She has eyes that see what you don't, a mind that assimilates information from a different perspective, a heart with sensitivities you do not possess, and a personality with strengths that offset your weaknesses. That's a built in protection for you. (p. 174)

An individual spouse allows the other spouse to become balanced by being a part of him or her. A spouse can help regulate the need to achieve fulfillment without unnecessary pain. As men and women, we are equal in partnership not just in marriage, but in every sphere of human endeavor.

8

Applying the Golden Rule and Developing Marital Automaticity

THE GOLDEN RULE
AND HOW IT APPLIES TO MARRIAGE

I HAVE WONDERED FOR a very long time if there is a golden rule for marriage. Recently I came across a suggestion for a golden rule of marriage. Harley (1997) stipulates that this should be "meet your spouse's needs as you would want your spouse to meet your needs" (p. 54). I am in disagreement with Harley's (1997) position because it is built on the principle of sum thinking and mere reciprocity.

The concept of reciprocity is a useful one but the current application of it to marriage needs to be revamped. The way that the term is being used externalizes need fulfillment, but product thinking internalizes the fulfillment of needs. In product thinking, reciprocity is guided by a type of thinking which allows for reciprocity to be seen as equal care within the self, which one knows will be affected by brokenness and finitude. However, in sum thinking, reciprocity becomes contaminated with preoccupation with "self."

When I started reflecting deeply on the old adage called the golden rule, I recognized that the same rule is applicable to marriage. The Golden Rule says "do unto others as you would have them do unto you." However, unlike Harley's (1997) stipulation when this is translated into marriage, it would be "do unto your partner as you would have your partner do unto you." However, to move away from the sum approach to the product approach discussed earlier, it should read, "Do unto yourself as you would like yourself do unto you."

In marriage, one has no time to think about reciprocity because when understood properly, one is really doing the thing for one's self. Therefore, one should stop thinking about reciprocity and fulfill one's responsibilities. It is important for both partners to internalize this nugget of truth in order to change their attitudes and behaviors that operate on the externalized reciprocal paradigm.

The golden rule of marriage must be clearly understood because it drives compassion. The golden rule motivates one to be compassionate. Whenever a proper understanding of the golden rule is internalized it strengthens compassion. One should love his or her partner beyond measure. In as much as one would want to receive from one's partner, one should give to one's partner. For example, a spouse should strive to love his or her partner more than the mind can fully comprehend. To love beyond measure implies that nothing will stop one from loving and even that which should cause one to stop loving, from a human perspective, will cause one to continue loving. One is always expecting one's partner to act in one's best interests so one always acts in his or her partner's best interests.

Doing unto one's partner as one would like a partner to do unto him or her indicates that there is always a need to serve one's partner. An individual should always make it a priority to look at how he or she can reciprocate that which her or she would like his or her partner to do for him or her and in turn does the same for the other partner. Partners should seek to understand each other and treat each other out of that understanding so that when the golden rule is applied in all its complexities, it allows for the full expression of marital love. Whenever something is done for a partner, the action is done unto one's self. When one loves one's partner, it is one's self that one is showing love. One might think that he or she does not have the capacity to accept one's partner beyond measure, but this is highly possible given the basis on which authentic love is built as previously discussed.

Accepting one's partner beyond measure will prevent dysfunctional marital problems by producing healing behaviors when human brokenness and finitude negatively affect the quality of love being received. It will cause a person to forgive and be committed to one's partner despite his or her weaknesses. When one accepts what one has, one will not seek for what one doesn't have through devotion to each other. One should make use of what she or he has and work on improving it in the ways that he or she is able to make changes. The first step in loving one's partner beyond measure is to accept one's partner without marital condition. A spouse empowers his or her partner through love by accepting his or her partner beyond measure. A feeling of acceptance of each other produces a feeling of liberation.

AUTOMATICITY AND HOW IT APPLIES TO MARRIAGE

It has been said repeatedly that marriage is hard work. However, one should reflect on whether or not this comment is a myopic vision of what marriage should be. In reflecting, the conclusion is a bankrupt paradigm and attitude. It seems to be based on a rather poor practice than hard work. When I was learning to drive, it was difficult to focus on the road and the things around as well as the controls at the same time. As my skills developed, I was able to drive without paying conscious attention to the controls. As an "experienced" driver, I am still learning to drive as I face new situations. However, because I have marshaled important driving skills, I am able to apply my knowledge to new situations. I have developed automaticity in driving through years of experience. Practice on the road has given me the ability to become more alert when the need arises.

One needs to develop marital skills so that there is a high level of automaticity in one's relationship. Marital automaticity is a new paradigm for building healthy marriages as the way that one deals with certain things in a relationship (marriage) must become second nature. In comparison, learning to drive before automaticity results, one has to intentionally do things in one's marriage before it becomes second nature. Intentionality is so important that a method for improving relationships has been developed. Clinebell (1984) suggests four steps of intentionality: 1) identify and affirm the strengths in the relationship; 2) identify the growing edge of the relationship (areas in which one needs to grow); 3) intentionally increase the mutual satisfaction of the relationship (choosing to meet each other's needs based on areas in which one needs to grow); and 4) implement the change plan. The rationale behind this concept is that there is the need to pay attention to the areas in the relationship where one needs to grow while celebrating the good things that are happening. However, intentionality must become automaticity in the form of a purpose-driven marriage that is moving from intentionality to automaticity.

Note carefully that the longer one drives a vehicle, the more familiarity one achieves with the vehicle. This translates into an understanding of one's partner as time progresses. Marriage does not have to be hard work for a "long time" if one builds the right foundation as well as builds on that foundation. Marital automaticity is built on knowledge not on ignorance. Education is a key to marital satisfaction and those who take the time to be educated will reap the prerequisites for success.

It is very difficult to try learning to drive a vehicle that is not roadworthy. An individual needs to get the vehicle passed by an engineer before learning to drive it. Proper tools will give a person an advantage in learning proper driving skills. This principle can be applied to the need to ensure that one's partner is fit and proper for a long-term relationship, through participation in necessary counseling, before trying to develop the skills of relating, leading to automaticity. Learning with the wrong tool can give a person the illusion that he or she knows when he or she doesn't have a clue. The real thing always works differently from that which needs repair and can get worse if it is not fixed in a timely way.

9

The Master Plan of Marriage and the Marital Love Cycle

THE MASTER PLAN OF MARITAL LOVE

THE MASTER PLAN OF marital love is to automatically love a partner authentically after love matures through the love cycle. It also requires that love be all-embracing and all-encompassing in order to understand human brokenness and bondage and to develop compassion and a willingness to forgive. Authentic love has no place for a hardened heart and for an unforgiving attitude or selfish ambition. It requires that product thinking consumes one's thoughts in relation to one's partner.

Although the intention is for authentic love to permeate one's marriage, being maintained automatically, the cycle sometimes starts over. This is a part of the maintenance of authentic love, when one keeps on loving authentically one is bound to remember where he or she started. Wheat (1983) concurs in his affirmation that "Lovers never seem to tire of sharing tender reminiscences about their love affair: the intrigue of first meeting . . . the sweet moment when they confessed their caring . . . the thrill of their surrender to each other" (p. 46).

Reflection takes a person back to connectedness and sets the marital love cycle in motion. The cycle is also set in motion when hard times impact the relationship or there are challenges or conflicts. Whenever the cycle is properly worked through the relationship tends to get stronger. The master plan of marriage requires a working through of the marital love to increase the potential to be a greater lover.

A person cannot truly say he or she loves when things to prevent an individual from loving become an obstacle as a person's true love is demonstrated when there are reasons to stop loving but there is a choice of love. Love for a partner should not be circumstantial but to love beyond measure. Whenever an individual loves in this way there will be a compulsion to be the best to the partner at every level, regardless of marital shortcomings or "non-comings"!

In the master plan of marriage, an intention is to love based on a decision to keep on loving. The desire to love will cause the growth of good marital skills and to intentionally apply them to the marital relationship. A decision to continue loving forces a person to love so much that it becomes a part of daily lifestyle. When one says that "nothing can stop me from loving my partner," one actually means absolutely nothing, which is a commitment to express love to one's partner regardless of the person's reactions, actions or responses.

The Marital Love Cycle

There are many family life cycle theories that I have come across in reading and training, but to date, I have not discovered any marital love cycle! In a cycle, if something is wrong with some of the gears or parts of the cycle, the cycle will not work properly. Although a person will be able to get some of the work done if the cycle is not working well, the person will have problems getting the more difficult part of the job done because it requires more power or better working conditions.

In this conceptualization of the marital love cycle, all the parts are important, which means that there will be times when some parts might not be consciously used. The parts must be intact so that when there is need for them, they are readily available. Figure 3 presents a diagram of the marital love cycle.

The Marital love cycle has six stages which results in connection with one's partner to automatically care for the total well-being of the person in the marital relationship. The presentation of the marital love cycle is to show how authentic love develops and automaticity develops to interact and to maintain balance to deal with challenges or conflict.

A cycle comprises one complete turn, interval turns or continuous turns. In this marital love cycle, it is both a complete turn along with interval turns. The intervals may be triggered by circumstances in the relationship which may lead to reflection. The interval cycles are important because they allow for reflection that strengthens the marriage. It is said that it is important to remember where one is coming from, as to remember where one is coming from, can give the drive to keep on going. When individuals consider how far they have come as a couple, it gives them reason to hold on and to keep on going.

Marital Love Cycle

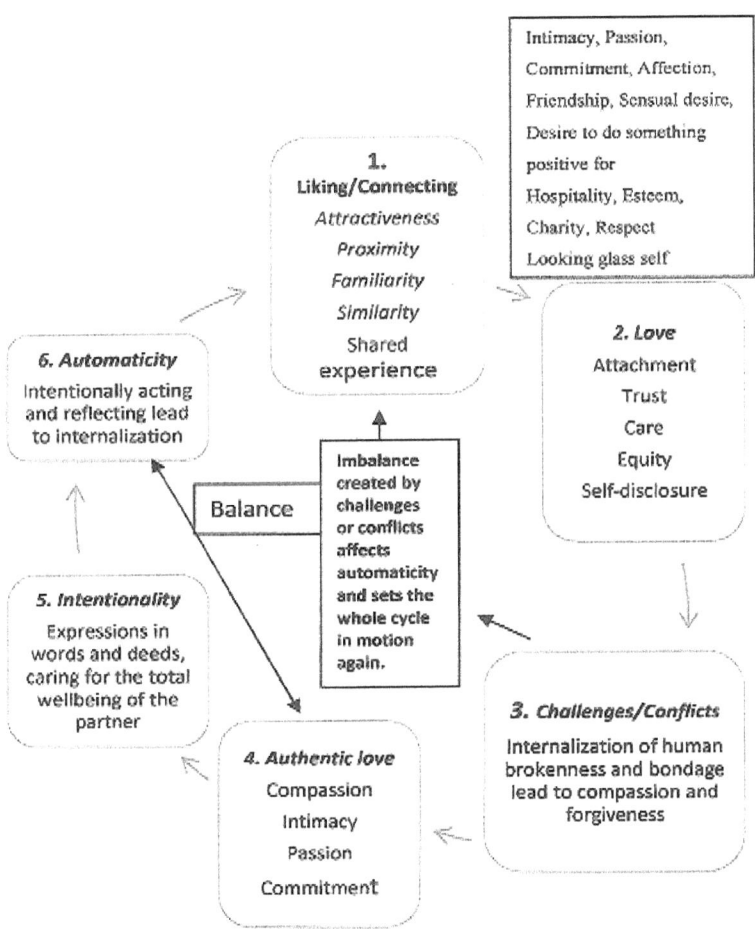

Figure 3

Liking/Connecting

It is a great miracle how a person meets his or her life partner. The miracle is great probably not because one met someone who lived in a far country but that the person is someone who lived within walking or driving distance. This is so interesting as a person is more likely to marry someone with whom she or he is closely connected by various shared experiences or situations. It is amazing how the person with whom one probably did not have any interest can become a lifelong partner!

As noted earlier, social psychologists believe that there are a number of factors that impact on a person liking another person. It is argued that physical attraction plays a role, but it is not as important, because people tend to be attracted to persons based on social affiliation. Physical attractiveness is not a major factor in someone liking a person because although physical attractiveness plays a part, it does not carry as much weight as some other factors. The saying that beauty is in the eyes of the beholder may shed some light on this. Could this be based on the beholder's comparison of the person with self? Social psychologists have demonstrated that this is so (Myers, 2005).

Social psychologists further contend that proximity and familiarity are even more important than attractiveness. An individual is more likely to marry someone with whom her or his path crosses frequently. The proximity between one person and the other person makes the person available. Availability leads to familiarity because as an individual gets to know the other person, interconnectedness is formed.

Individuals' close proximity facilitate the important ingredient of getting to know one another. Individuals became familiar with each other as they are able to trust based on knowing the other person. They probably had some liking for each other or no liking but as time went by, given proximity and familiarity, they grew to like each other. They pursued each other (sorry ladies, he was not the only one pursuing!) until they finally settled down together. Persistence pays off; give thanks for the power of proximity and familiarity.

It is said that opposites attract. However, experience and research have helped to clarify that similarity is a powerful tool in the liking paradigm leading to love. People will marry persons with whom they have things in common. Individuals get married to their spouses because they are similar in many important ways (religion, values, background, either professionals or skilled workers, food, similar views on children, on marriage, and the list goes on). When one stops to think about how similar she or he is to one's partner as against how different she or he is, the list of similarities will dwarf the list of differences.

Shared experiences have a powerful effect on bringing persons together. This shared experience was facilitated by individuals' proximity and possibly similarity. Individuals met each other because of the nature of their occupation (similarity) or because they lived in the same neighborhood or their path crossed frequently due to increased mobility and technology (proximity). Individuals had shared experiences because they attended a class or school together or they knew the relatives or friends of each other. When individuals think of those shared experiences that brought them together, they experience pleasant memories.

Love

We have established that attraction can lead to love and various factors contribute to attraction. Love does not develop in a vacuum. It develops based on the shared experiences of persons. Love is hard to define; it is easier for one to experience it. It should thrill one's heart to know that in marriage one is able to love completely, expressing all the dimensions of love in one direction. This is real authentic love.

Individuals move from liking their partners to loving their partners when they are moved in their hearts and minds at a very deep level. It is not just a head decision but a heart decision. Persons' thinking and emotions produce their loving behavior. Persons find this decision hard to break because their hearts are involved. A mere rational decision is easy to be broken, but when persons' hearts are in it they find it difficult to convince their hearts to compromise the decision in any way.

When one started loving, one did so on the basis that one found that one could not live without one's partner (attachment without being enmeshed), cared so much for one's partner that one was prepared to do just about anything for him or her, and trusted one's partner so much that one gave oneself to one's partner, and confided in him or her. This kind of mental process and decision, packed with emotions, influenced one's behaviors. One started expressing love to one's partner in various ways; expressions were evident in words and deeds.

A number of things impacted on the love that a person developed for her or his partner. A person felt intimacy (closeness) that caused him or her to share a lot in many and varied ways. A person's passion (desires) caused him or her to want to be with one's partner even just to know that he or she is there for him or her. A person's commitment (willingness to be around forever) caused him or her to work through challenges and remain faithful. A person's head and heart decision caused him or her to develop perserverance. Individuals became truly in love as their intimacy, passion and commitment fuse together.

One's unconscious synergy of love, in the various dimensions of it, impacted on one's love. Individuals began to be passionate, committed, intimate, and compassionate. They always desired to act in the best interest of their partner and to be their best friend. Their love became all-embracing and all-encompassing.

CHALLENGES OR CONFLICTS

Every long-standing relationship has gone through trials and tests. Trials of what one says and tests of what one has learned. A healthy relationship is not based on the absence of conflict but on how conflicts are dealt with when they arise. Balswick and Balswick (1999) support the claim that conflict is not necessarily absent from healthy relationships in that "conflict is a normal part of intimate relationships" (p. 254). It is not saying that conflict makes up the relationship because this would not be a good foundation on which to build a marriage. However, given the differences between the two persons who come together, conflict allows for clarity and facilitates assimilation (understanding areas of similarity) and accommodation (understanding areas of difference). Trust develops as one understands his or her similarities and differences.

The challenges that an individual faced in a relationship allowed reflection on his or her partner's weaknesses as well as one's own weaknesses. This enabled a person to recognize that he or she is not perfect and neither is his or her partner. A person has to reflect on this at a deeper level until it touches the heart deep down. This internalization will allow a person to truly understand human brokenness and bondage. One is forced to admit that in the same way one does not do or say the right thing at times, so it is with one's partner. Just as how someone wants to do good but is misunderstood at times, so it is with the partner.

An understanding of the struggle of humanity, by reflecting on one's own struggles, will allow for compassion. This compassion is hinged on recognition that a man or woman is in need of help. One is compassionate because he or she knows that when people want to do good, evil presents itself. The compassionate attitude will allow a person to forgive and maintain the relationship through an understanding of the struggle that humanity is experiencing. A person is able to forgive when there is a love for a partner who is unwilling to let go. Forgiveness is cultivated by a mindset of forgiveness and a heart of compassion (Young, 2003).

Authentic Love

One may say she or he loves, but the trials and tests are necessary to cement one's love. Trials and tests allow a person to reflect on his or her brokenness and bondage with that of his or her partner in order to develop compassion. This could be what accounts for passionate love becoming affectionate love after the hot period in the relationship (Myers, 2005). A person is able to love not on the basis of the perfection of his or her partner but on a decision to love after a proper understanding that the partner in the relationship may fail in the same way as the other person.

Authentic love develops when a person is able to love despite experiencing confusion of feelings towards one's partner. This kind of love consistently moves a person's mind, will, thoughts, feelings, and actions in a positive direction. It allows a person to give even when he or she thinks he or she is not receiving.

There can be no authentic love without compassion and there can be no compassion without forgiveness. An individual learns to be compassionate through the conflicts and challenges in an intimate relationship. Persons will become compassionate and consummate partners in an attempt to keep intimacy, passion and commitment going. Intimacy, passion and commitment continue to be positively impacted by the characteristics of love in order to produce authentic love, which is held together by compassion. Compassion is the component that holds individuals' love together, for without compassion love can become fragmented because of human brokenness and bondage.

Intentionality

Authentic love is responsible for causing a consuming desire to care for the total well-being of one's partner through a commitment to always do that which needs to be done, regardless of how demanding it may be. An individual's product thinking as discussed earlier, will intensify an insatiable desire to satisfy the needs of the partner in the relationship, knowing that he or she is really doing it for himself or herself. A person no longer thinks reciprocity but is instead focused on fulfilling his or her responsibilities.

A person needs to continuously practice to be a good lover by loving in words and deeds as an expression of one's love. One is never satisfied with love not being expressed as love is always open and never hidden. One knows that love requires good practice in order for one to master it through commitment to learn the art and science of love and also to apply it deliberately and without reservations.

Automaticity

The love cycle is complete when one automatically starts caring for the total well-being of one's partner that it becomes a habit. An individual can develop a pattern of expressing love in words and deeds for it to penetrate one's total life. When love is a part of one's commitment it is easier to love. It becomes second nature to care for the well-being of one's partner.

Automaticity does not prevent intentionality and one has to learn new skills and develop new habits of relating to each other on the marital journey. Intentionality still comes into play when a relationship needs something different in the form of both stability and change. Intentionality allows a person to deal with those changes as she or he goes through the life cycle.

One only needs to practice the art and science of love so that it becomes a part of one's nature to love one's partner as a way of life. Loving a partner is to be done authentically so that a blessing will be received in loving as a way of life and not one's bane to not love consistently or failing frequently. A person's thoughts should become so saturated with what needs to be done in expressing love to a partner that the emotions and actions automatically fall into place. Automaticity in the authentic love relationship should be guided by product thinking and egalitarianism.

10

Servanthood in Male-Female Relationship

THE THOUGHT OF BEING a servant can cause many persons to cringe, given humanity's infamous history of slavery and patriarchal legacy. A proper understanding of the term "servanthood" is foundational to product thinking and egalitarianism in male-female relationships. An egalitarian relationship is maintained by daily unconditional service to each other based on product thinking. Tan (2006) observes in his work with couples that only a few of them enter the male-female relationship with a commitment to make servanthood a key priority of their lives together (p. 151). Although space will not allow for a full treatment of this subject, a few observations and connections articulated by the author are warranted.

The word servant has both negative and positive connotations. In the negative sense it refers to one of mean condition, lacking the basic necessities of life, while the positive relates to a devotion to serve or pledged to serve. When the term servant is used with a positive connotation, it refers to one who chooses to serve others. Servanthood is the combination of the noun "servant" and the noun suffix "hood." With a positive connotation, servanthood therefore refers to the state, condition, quality or character of one who serves others. Servanthood in marriage is a commitment to follow the product thinking principle and the egalitarian philosophy in daily unconditional service to one's partner. Servanthood carries the force of the Latin Theological term caritas which refers to "self-giving love" (Muller, 1985, p. 60).

Servanthood in a male-female relationship has been negatively affected by entrenched patriarchal thinking and fuelled the theological debate on female submission. The debate is centered on female submission instead of mutual authentic submission, which creates problematic social structures due to a male-centered theology (Parsons, 1996). Both mutual submission and female submission are taught in the Christian Bible (Ephesians 5:21–33). Furthermore, female submission is predicated on mutual submission, which suggests that mutual submission is the guiding principle in the text. Bilezikian (1985) observes that Ephesians 5:21 deals with reciprocal servanthood, which, in essence, upstaged the then dominant culture of patriarchy and enforced egalitarianism. The common practice of separating mutual submission from female submission in the "submission" debate seems to overlook exegetically sound principles.

The concept of mutual submission is negatively affected by the theological concept of headship. This is challenging to resolve because of the treatment of mutual submission and female submission in the same passage of Scripture (Ephesians 5:21–33). The Greek word "kephalee" (used 75 times in the Greek New Testament), which is translated to mean head in the Christian Bible, is used literally, metaphorically or figuratively (Bauer, 1958/1979, p. 430). The term is flexible and should be interpreted in context with the force of the text.

The term "head" in Ephesians 5:23 may be either figurative or metaphorical. When it is used figuratively it denotes superior rank of living beings, which is unlikely to be the interpretation in the context, given the guiding principle of mutual submission on which the statement is predicated. When it is used metaphorically it denotes authority or direction (Vine, 1966; Rogers and Rogers, 1998). This is the more likely interpretation when the emphasis is placed on direction.

Bilezikian (1985) notes that from the metaphor of Christ as head of the church in the text, his headship is defined in terms of saviorhood, servanthood and nurturance (p. 158). The "headship" of the husband must be interpreted in the same way that the headship of Christ is explained in the text, not on authority but on direction in terms of protecting, serving and empowering. It is the provider-servant role of the husband that is inaugurated as a paradigm shift from the patriarchal history (Bilezikian, 1998, p. 162). In the context of Ephesians 5:21–33, the author realizes that the metaphor breaks down at certain points and so indicates that it is a mystery, and he is referring to Christ and the church. The important points in the text are in verse 21, which has to do with mutual submission, and verse 33, which has to do with love of wife as self in relation to the husband and respect of husband in relation to wife (Rogers and Rogers, 1998). Love and respect in the text are based on mutual submission and therefore result in true servanthood.

Mutual submission makes it imperative for couples to learn to serve each other with a servant's heart motivated by the noble idea to serve others. Benner (2003) notes that "lovers demonstrated their love by doing what each other wants" (p. 64). Love becomes action oriented instead of feeling generated. Covey (1989, 2004) notes that reactive people make love a feeling while proactive people make it a verb because they believe that love is about the sacrifices one makes in the giving of self that actualizes the value of love so that feelings become subordinated to values (p. 80). Love becomes character-based and principle-centered reflected in the modeling of true servanthood, which makes it impossible to love without serving.

Servanthood is important for marital satisfaction. For example, instead of giving off negative energy an individual should choose to side-step a partner's weaknesses by being proactive instead of reactive. Product thinking generates the passion for servanthood in a male-female relationship while egalitarianism drives the mission for the fruition of the vision of equality. The theological concept of mutual submission supports the egalitarian ideal, which is tantamount to servanthood generated by product thinking.

Serving a partner in marriage may be engaged in from various paradigms. For service to be considered true servanthood it has to be motivated by product thinking and egalitarianism. Figure 4 shows the four quadrants of service along the lines of egalitarianism and product thinking.

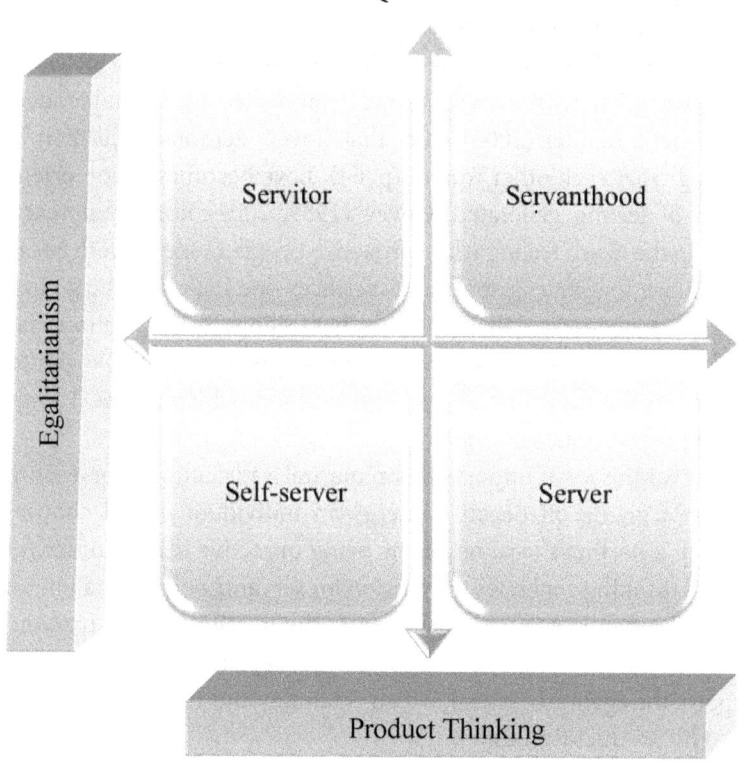

Figure 4

The self-server is a person who engages in service that is self-centered. There is no internalization of the product thinking and egalitarian philosophy and principle. The attitude of this person is tantamount to a moral stage of development based on self-interest alone. The server is one who believes in product thinking but is trapped in the patriarchal approach to service, whereas the servitor does not believe in product thinking but is pushed by circumstances to engage in an egalitarian approach for the balancing of the relationship. These two kinds of services move in the right direction to a certain degree but fail to be high on both dimensions. Therefore, the servitor feels like a slave because (s)he is merely serving because of the new trends whereas the server feels like a fool because (s)he is shackled by the patriarchal legacy.

High egalitarianism and product thinking result in servanthood as a kind of service that finds joy in service (Covey, 2004, p. 292). True servanthood puts service above self. Servanthood results in attending to the well-being of a spouse in making positive contributions for the empowerment of the spouse as a way of making daily deposits of unconditional love (Covey, 1989, 2004). It becomes a joy to serve as one finds security in service. It is a commitment to the principles of product thinking and egalitarianism that one has rationally understood. This represents a high stage of moral development.

DEMONSTRATING TRUE SERVANTHOOD

One of the hardest things to do is to serve when an individual would rather be served. It is even more difficult to serve when a person doesn't think that the recipient deserves it. Remember that in marriage, this kind of thinking is 'sum thinking' that is bankrupt. Rather, product thinking causes a spouse to remember that he or she is doing it for himself or herself and so the pleasure to serve even when one doesn't feel like serving will benefit the person directly or indirectly. When a spouse serves his or her partner, it always benefits him or her in return.

As a spouse, have you ever wondered if your partner would just do what you require of him or her at a given moment? If this has been your experience it may very well be the experience of your partner. A spouse may discover what areas his or her partner would want to be served in by asking his or her partner how he or she would like to be treated. Whenever one asks, one should be prepared to do whatever is requested.

A spouse can serve her or his partner's goals and support them by becoming passionate about the partner's dreams and aspirations. A person should internalize his or her partner's dreams and aspirations so that they affect his or her life positively. One must be committed to serve a partner with the belief that by providing support of one's partner, he or she is supporting himself or herself. A spouse becomes his or her partner's cheerleader by knowing and supporting a partner's dreams and aspirations.

For service to the partner, one needs to postpone gratifying his or her other desires and wishes and make service to his or her partner a priority. It is sometimes hard to pause what one is doing to serve where one is needed. However, if one interprets the situation as an emergency, one will need to respond immediately.

Providing service is a metaphor of driving a motor vehicle on a long journey and the gas tank is running low. The driver reached a service station but decided not to stop although she or he does not know where the next one is going to be. The motorist continued driving only to run out of fuel and suffer the consequences. The operator of the vehicle suffered the consequences due to the fact that she or he did not treat the situation as an emergency when he or she should have.

In relating this metaphor to marriage, a spouse needs to interpret his or her partner's calls as emergencies. If one does not, one will suffer the consequences of a failure to respond to a partner's needs by radically transforming the relationship through product thinking from intentionality to automaticity.

A Recipe for Daily Service to Your Partner

In order for it to become automatic for a spouse to serve his or her partner on a daily basis, a spouse needs to intentionally do some things to foster this. The following is a suggested list of things that an individual should make a part of his or her daily service list in serving a partner.

1. Reflecting in the morning—spend time reflecting and meditating in the morning before parting company. This reflection should give the couple a sense of what the day will be like. This should enable the couple to pick up the concerns and challenges. This could lead the couple to pray about the situation and further support each other throughout the day through telephone conversations and e-mails. A spouse could directly ask his or her partner how he or she wants to be served for the day.

2. Communicate during the day—one should take time out to speak with one's partner at least once during the day on the telephone. A spouse could support the spouse with a phone call following up by an e-mail stating how much he or she appreciated speaking to his or her partner and the plans for both of them later.

3. Debrief in the evening—spend some time reflecting on the day's activities, successes and disappointments by reassuring in love by upholding, admonishing, affirming, encouraging, edifying

and praying. A spouse should ask a partner how he or she wants to be served or treated as they debrief and to carry out requests, despite the personal challenge. The man should always be open with finances so that his partner will know the possibilities, and so he can interpret her requests as fair. The way in which one's partner wants to be served is always thought of as an emergency as serving a partner's needs is a part of how one makes his or her partner feel special.

4. Be close at nights—a couple should never let the day go by without touching each other meaningfully. This does not necessarily mean sex but the communication of warmth and friendship which is an indication of how they are bonding together. A couple should not allow unresolved issues to keep them apart, but instead ensure that issues are resolved before retiring to sleep. Go to sleep at peace so that it will not affect the start of a new day.

Become your Partner's Chief Servant

During the dating period, a couple would respond positively to each other's request to impress each other. Similarly, marriage partners need to continue to impress their partners every day by being each other's chief servant through an ability to bless his or her partner. Wheat and Perkins (1980) affirm this position by stating that a spouse blesses by bestowing practical benefits upon a partner by simply doing kind things just to please, not as a duty, but as a gift of blessing as a daily part of marriage (p. 178). A spouse serves a partner's needs by always being a blessing not a curse and to act in the best interest of the partner.

Service is essential to satisfy the marital bonds. In marriage, a partner cannot use the other partner because when one serves a partner one is serving one's self. As an individual serves, there should never be a thought that one is being taken advantage of or that one is being taken for granted as love always requires action. A spouse should always ask what she or he is doing to make a partner see that she or he loves her or him. When a partner experiences love, there will be feelings of appreciation due to the other person giving the best in service.

Tan (2006) notes that marital partners must have a servanthood attitude as marital research generally supports the benefits of sacrifice or servanthood in marriage (p. 158). This kind of sacrifice in marriage does not suggest endangering one's life in extreme situations of abuse but to allow for separation in order to get professional help. Servanthood in marriage requires sensitivity to the needs of a partner and a willingness to meet those needs. It is a willingness to give 100 percent despite the other party not getting 100 percent in return.

Become the Best Love Maker

Becoming a great love maker is a learning process and of progressive discoveries. Wheat and Wheat (1997) observe that several hindrances blocked this learning process in the past. Wheat and Wheat (1997) feel that young couples were brainwashed by the romantic novels and movies that suggest that sexual satisfaction comes naturally, and many people have been defensive about their knowledge and skills as lovers, they feel that they must pretend to know it all or else admit to lack of sexual prowess (p. 79). Wheat and Wheat (1997) further acknowledge that this problematic trend is changing as couples are now seeking counseling on the issue instead of leaving their relationship to the trial an error method that may or may not lead to sexual satisfaction. The burgeoning field of sex therapy supports the authors' observations of changing attitudes.

A married couple should ensure satisfaction of the sexual appetite of each other as a vital part of commitment in marriage and servanthood. Marital relationship should involve satisfying the sexual desires to avoid infidelity and frustration in the marriage. One needs to keep one's "shop" open and people . . . oops, men have a way of checking out the "'bar" (refers to a place that mainly sells alcohol, which is consumed immediately most of the time and more purchased until one is unable to continue drinking sometimes because of intoxication) when the "shop" (refers to a place where general food items are sold, especially basic food items) is closed. When men go to the "bar" there is no telling what state they will return in. One should strive to keep one's partner in one's "shop." A spouse should make her or his partner her or his only customer and ascertain and acquire the goods that are needed before demand.

Sexual relation in marriage is a part of servanthood in marriage. Sex can be compared to cuisine where a good meal needs time for proper preparation. Partners should take time to meet each other's sexual need just as how much work is involved in preparing a meal. Both partners should view sex as a metaphor of a meal in its preparation and the tantalizing enjoyment of consumption. When one learns the art, it gets much easier. Figure 5 outlines my conceptualization of the cycle of love making that could help improve the love making process of a marital couple. The information chronicled earlier on the historicity of human sexuality is also a tremendous asset.

Cycle of Love Making

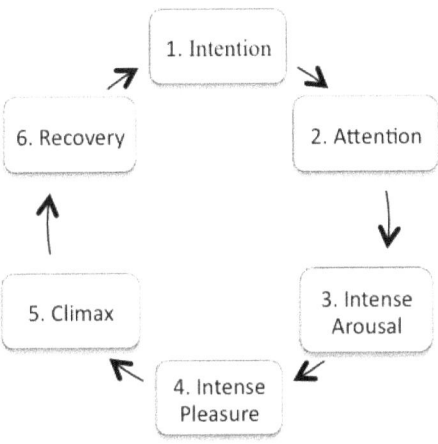

Figure 5

Love making starts with one's intention to make love with a partner with the aim of strengthening the marital bond. Second, one should start giving her or his partner attention by engaging in meaningful conversations to clear the mind and relax through psychological preparation by dealing with issues that are unresolved. Setting the mood by having dinner out or sending a bouquet or a love letter among other things are important precursors to love making.

Third, as one becomes intensely aroused, spending time caressing each other will involve the erotic zones. It is important to be familiar with the "moan" and "groan" erotic areas to encourage strong stimulation.

Fourth, an individual experiences intense pleasure by the insertion of the penis into the vagina by continuously stimulating each other through rhythmic movements of both partners. The rhythmic movements allow the penis to make contact with the clitoris or stimulation through the contraction of the clitoral hood as the vagina caresses the nerve endings of the penis and produces intense pleasure that both partners desire to continue in increasing intensity.

Fifth, climax or orgasm is the result of continuous movement, where both partners reach the point of sexual release. It is known as the apogee of sexual intercourse and is a very pleasurable feeling that can cause one to feel weak due to an ecstatic experience. It is important that the male exercises control in order to ensure the female's orgasm due to the fact that both partners may not climax at the same time but should get maximum satisfaction from the experience.

The male should facilitate the female's multiple orgasm after climaxing if she desires this. An addendum is crucial at this point because of variations in the female sexual response cycle discussed earlier. The female may not be open to engage in the physical movement, mental concentration and releasing in search of sexual release. Therefore, if she decides not to climax (although she might change her mind) her decision should be respected. The experience can nevertheless be fulfilling as long as the female still joins the male in the sex act. Harley (1997) agrees with this view in his claim that some females:

> Confided in . . . [him] that they really don't find reaching climax worth the effort it takes to do so. They have reached it at times, but they are quite happy with the sex act without orgasm and wish their husbands would not frequently pressure them to climax . . . [he] generally encourage men to let their wives decide whether or not to experience climax. (p. 51)

Wheat and Wheat (1997) disagree with this view. From their perspective, mutual orgasm and multiple orgasms should be the result of sexual intercourse. Given what was discovered in the history of human sexuality narrated earlier, it is not without good reason that the proposal for the wife to decide whether or not to climax is being advocated in this product thinking paradigm. Mutual orgasm and multiple orgasm for the wife should be the goal but not necessary the result.

Finally, the recovery stage involves relaxing where partners should use this time for relaxation and touching each other lovingly. A couple should also express gratitude for satisfying each other sexually in such a remarkable way. The couple may be tired but should ensure reflection on the experience with each other. It is important that a couple be honest with the sexual experience so that improvements can be made where necessary. It is not embarrassing to talk about the sex act.

It is important for a spouse to learn as much as possible about human physiology as it will help to properly massage and stimulate a partner. There is a major difference between the physiology of males and females that needs to be borne in mind, especially the psychological or emotional female response. After a couple has climaxed, the female might still be able to climax soon thereafter, while the male needs time to build up another erection. The male can continue to give stimulation to the female if she desires through creative touching which would suggest that the resolution phase for the female may be delayed. It would be helpful to review the chapter on the historicity of human sexuality at this point.

Make Your Partner Feel Special through Servanthood

In relationships, love is the issue most discussed through expressions of love or disappointment of a lack of expression. As a marriage partner, an individual should strive to ensure that the discussion is centered on the appreciation for expressions of love. Appreciation and thankfulness for expressions of love is strengthened when one makes it a habit to act lovingly towards his or her partner on a daily basis. The other partner should feel proud that attention is being given to enhance the model of servanthood.

When an individual is dating, he or she tries to do things to make the person feel special. The dating relationship should continue in marriage, and as one continues to "date" his or her partner, he or she will continuously look for gifts to take for the other. Couples should continue to use words of affirmation and write love letters in the form of cards for her or his partner. Too much time should not be allowed to elapse before writing his or her partner a love letter.

A spouse makes his or her partner feel special by the spending of quality and quantity time to allow a spouse to know how to treat a partner and what is happening in his or her partner's life. One will remain connected to one's partner by spending quality time and a person will feel special when he or she feels connected to his or her spouse.

A partner will feel special when the other person is committed to share one's total life with his or her partner. Sharing is a powerful way to prevent distancing and hardening of the heart as every area of life should be shared, including self-disclosure, which is important in deepening love (Myers, 2005). An individual's successes, disappointments, challenges, dreams, aspirations and plans should be shared for feedback.

A spouse will make his or her partner feel special by thanking him or her for being the kind of person that he or she is. One should make his or her partner know that he or she cannot do without him or her by emphasizing that he or she is going to love his or her partner more and more. A spouse should thank his or her partner for putting up with him or her and remember that he or she is not perfect. A partner will need to keep working in the relationship in order to meet a partner's needs and by so doing really meet his or her own needs.

A husband continues to make his wife feel special by remaining chivalrous, seeking to always remember each other's special days and events. For example, a husband could volunteer to be his wife's chauffeur to or from work or to take out his partner for dinner or lunch as often as possible.

A husband can call her at work and, on occasion, send a bouquet even when there is no special event. And remember to protect her from the outside world as well as from family, including her own children. McDowell (1996) emphasizes the importance of demanding respect from one's children for one's wife. A husband should let his children know that he loves their mother and will not tolerate them speaking to his wife disrespectfully. Don't allow anyone to disrespect her in front of her or behind her without standing up for her.

A person needs to learn to enjoy what a partner enjoys even if it is not a favorite activity. When a spouse spends time to learn the activity, it will make one's partner feel special because the person will know the partner is doing it for him or her. An individual should not remind a partner about past failings but should make a commitment to notice any improvements and to celebrate them. One should make his or her partner feel special with a combination of words and deeds along with humor appropriately being used so that the partner may enjoy some good laughter. A spouse does not have to take everything so seriously but be playful with each other.

An individual should be committed to support the partner's career goals and life plan. For example, if a partner identifies something that needs to be worked on, one should be willing to get counseling. A spouse should never let his or her partner feel inferior by just rejecting suggestions and a husband should ensure that he never let his wife feel inferior by being domineering. In addition, a wife should never let her husband feel inferior because she earns more money.

In a relationship, suggestions should never be rejected; they must always be processed where praise for one's partner is essential, whatever he or she does well or was bold enough to attempt. A spouse ought to give credit where credit is due and should not forget to mention his or her partner on special occasions or events. A spouse ought not to make unreasonable demands of his or her partner but instead should avoid being mechanical in compliments. Social psychologists have discovered that it is more powerful to say that something does not fit as nicely as something else, than to keep on saying that everything looks good (Myers, 2005).

The Healing Power of Relationship

A spouse causes his or her partner to feel special through the areas of intimacy that he or she seeks to develop in the marriage. Social psychologists have recognized the value of relationships and the unique value of a healthy marriage (Myers, 2005; Feldman, 2005; Santrock, 2005). A high-quality relationship has the power to heal emotional hurts and pains and the power to give the strength to cope and hope in times of frustration. Relationship is vital even in psychotherapy, where a kind of relationship that has healing power for emotional hurts must be created.

When one communicates with her or his partner, the parties should feel something different from the communication process. A spouse should feel special based on how her or his partner treats the relationship. The marital relationship is a very important component of life as a spouse ought to avoid being casual about her or his partner's concerns. For example, spending hours watching television or talking on the telephone, and treating a partner as last priority. One should be careful with the amount of time that is spent with the children and the limited time that is spent with a partner. A marriage partner ought not to allow his or her actions to cause his or her partner to feel like a loner.

Unresolved issues of the past can surface even when a person is madly in love. One should not blame one's partner for how his or her unresolved issues are affecting the relationship. When one is feeling loved, whatever is affecting him or her will surface because it wants to be positively affected by love. However, the spirit in which unresolved feelings are dealt with can block the power of a relationship to heal.

Therefore, a person can make a partner feel special by engaging together in counseling to deal with one's unresolved issues. Nothing will block the giving and receiving of love in one's relationship when personal issues have been resolved.

The importance of marital preparation, given the possibility of adjustment problems, is underscored by Davidson (1992) who states that the union of a male and female with different family backgrounds and varied past experiences will cause adjustment problems when they begin to share life together but if the stresses can be anticipated before the union takes place, the adjustment process is likely to be much easier in marriage (p. 7). If it is so important to prepare for adjustment problems, as narrated by Davidson (1992), without preparation, struggles can be experienced in marriage with issues that could have been avoided. The purpose of premarital counseling then can be summed up as helping couples understand themselves, their partners, and the institution of marriage. Premarital counseling then is an authentic sounding board for evaluating one's strengths and weaknesses as well as those of a partner and the individual's expectations. A lack of premarital counseling may be compensated for by partners taking the time to talk with a professional counselor as a married couple.

A couple should deliberately plan to do things together to make each other feel special throughout the year. The couple should take the time at the start of each year to make a list of at least ten important things that they would like to do together for the year. Two separate lists can be made and then combine the lists to ensure that a couple will plan special times together. Therefore, a marriage will get better when partners spend time together and treat each other like a best friend.

11

Applying the Concepts of Product Thinking, Egalitarianism and Authentic Love

PREVENT YOUR HEART FROM BECOMING HARD

A PERSON'S HEART BECOMES hard when there is no internalization of the components of love. Hurt and negative vibes will build tension, resulting in the rejection of a partner. In analyzing a relationship in which one believes that his or her needs are not being met, one becomes dissatisfied with a partner. Unmet emotional needs is the number one recipe to harden a person's heart towards a partner and to prevent further difficulties a person should take steps to deal with it immediately. The antidote to prevent the hardening of the heart is called product thinking. Product thinking leads to thanksgiving and a commitment to continue serving and fostering the relationship to avoid rationality without emotionality. There is a great need for compassion in a relationship in order to deal with the shortcomings of one's partner in ways that keep the growing edge of the relationship alive to foster marital success.

A failure to forgive will result in a hardening of the heart but healing power in forgiveness should be a model of love. Love requires action, even the action of forgiveness, which must be offered when it is needed, not when it is asked for. Forgiveness is always needed because of human brokenness and bondage. Pritchard (2005) suggests three useful levels of forgiveness: rediscovering the humanity of the person who is responsible for one's hurt, deciding not to get even by surrendering one's right to do so, and changing one's feeling towards the person who caused the hurt. These three levels are important in the process of offering authentic forgiveness (p. 25).

A hardened heart is also fuelled by a tendency to match expressions over expectations. Therefore, to prevent one's heart from becoming hard, celebrate expressions and evaluate one's own expressions to avoid stalemate in the marriage. What one has is always more important than what one is hoping to get and which might not be realistic. An individual should not be bogged down with the absent but should strive to work with what is present and hope that the expectant will come.

Engage in Introspection

In order for a person to keep her or his heart from becoming hard it is important to engage in introspection. This allows a person to assess the self within a relationship. A person is able to objectively assess a relationship and process feelings because of a capacity for reflection. This will help in detoxification and cleansing the mind of all negative thoughts, feelings and emotional baggage.

When one engages in introspection, one is able to deal with situations early that will have the potential to damage an intimate relationship. Early detection and treatment of marital issues that are having a negative impact on a relationship are important in building a healthy marriage. Identifying and dealing with things that need to be dealt with will allow a person's energy to be directed in the right direction. If negative situations are not handled properly they will siphon off one's energy.

One cannot do proper introspection without learning to tell the truth. It is important for a person to tell himself or herself the truth about his or her relationship and must therefore ensure objectivity. Making sure that the introspection is also guided by product thinking would entail an individual constantly evaluating marriage to ensure stability and maintenance of the relationship. An individual should be moving from intentionality to automaticity in a relationship as marriage is dynamic. If one is not moving forward one is slipping backward.

Evaluate the Roles in Your Marriage

Roles are essential functions of every group as proper functioning requires teamwork. Teamwork requires the fulfillment of individual responsibility to achieve shared objective. McGee (1980) points out that:

> All small groups, including the family, appear to require two different types of leaders. These have been designated the instrumental and expressive leadership roles. Although fundamentally different, they complement one another in the context of the small group. In most families, the husband performs one and the wife performs the other . . . (p. 311)

McGee's (1980) observation suggests that leadership roles are important in a family. The instrumental leadership role has to do with the administrative functions (ensuring that behaviors allow for the achievement of goals). The expressive leadership role has to do with resolving the tensions that are caused by behavioral demands. These leadership roles are divided among husband and wife.

A degree of flexibility needs to exist in an egalitarian relationship so that both partners can function in different roles, although one partner might be predominant in a particular role. It is important to note in talking about roles that the concepts of female and male are biological, while the concepts of feminine and masculine are culturally defined attributes. A leadership role is not based on masculinity or femininity as a role construct in an egalitarian relationship because this kind of relationship is diametrically opposed to the patriarchal culture to which we have become enslaved.

A person's heart tends to get hard when it is felt that his or her needs are not being met. It is important for a person to evaluate the roles in marriage, especially expectations which are not being met because it is possible for a person to expect more than a partner expected. With the changing role of women and the blurring of sex roles, it is important to evaluate one's expectations with the roles that can be realistically assigned. McGee (1980) concludes that "adjusting sex roles . . . can have profound effects upon the performance of other family role patterns" (p. 313). Therefore, the need to move from patriarchy to egalitarianism cannot be overemphasized.

When the wife is working outside of the home the expectations have to be different than if she was working from home. The roles that one should expect one's partner to play should be directly related to the areas of change and stability in one's marriage. It is important to note the need for change in expectations. According to Shepard and Green (2001), "men in dual-employed marriages are generally unwilling to assume household responsibilities equal to those of their wives" (p. 375).

In an egalitarian marriage, there needs to be equity in every respect. Product thinking causes persons to be fair to each other. In dual career relationships, especially the household responsibilities cannot be left up to the woman. Husbands should not treat their wives like superwomen. There needs to be balance in childrearing responsibilities as a couple should support each other at every level. Therefore, there is no place for power struggle. Let us examine how one should evaluate marriage from developmental, sociological, and psychological perspectives.

From a developmental perspective, there is the need for companionship. McGee (1980) verifies that in companionship the emphasis is on sharing all experiences with a partner and so implies greater intimacy, equality of power, privacy from the scrutiny of kin and neighbors, and the stabilization of adult personalities (p. 315). There is a need for equality of power in genuine companionship.

Marriage will be affected by both normative and non-normative influences. The normative influences are those things that are a natural part of the stages of marriage and the non-normative are those things that are unique to a particular marriage that were unexpected. Sensitivity to these issues is critical if one is going to be able to offer the care and support within the marital relationship at crucial points. Familiarity with the family life cycle can help a person to be prepared for normative influences.

In the late 1950s, Duvall (as cited in Theories of Family Development, 2004) conceptualized the family life cycle as a sequential and developmental process that involve predictable and normative issues as the family evolves over the life cycle. The stages of the family life cycle based on the nuclear family, which was commonplace at the time, consist of eight stages:

> (1) married couple without children; (2) childbearing families (oldest child from birth to 30 months); (3) families with preschool children (oldest child from 2.5 to 6 years); (4) families with school-age children (oldest from 6 to 13 years); (5) families with adolescents (oldest from 13 to 20 years); (6) families that are launching children from the home (from first child to last child to leave home); (7) middle years including empty-nest syndrome to retirement; and (8) and aging families extending from retirement to the death of both spouses. (Theories of Family Development, 2004)

However, given the family dynamics in this generation, including later marriages, single parenting, divorce, remarriage, and dual career couples, the stages will be affected primarily by age of marriage and marital stability or instability.

Notwithstanding the uniqueness of family development in this era, one needs to be sensitive to critical periods in the marriage, including birth of children, launching of children from home, and retirement. Counseling might be helpful at these points. In a dual career family, the active involvement of the husband in childrearing is crucial. Chasteen and Kissman (2000) assert that a transformation of a paternal helper into a more egalitarian co-parental role results in mothers being relieved of the heavy nurturing/caretaking responsibilities and balance of family and co-provider roles with less stress (p. 239). This underscores the necessity for an egalitarian relationship, which is further strengthened by Schnittger and Bird's (1990) study. The study concluded that the structure and constrains of the work environment and its incentives usually result in career commitment that involves long hours on career-related tasks especially in early career stages. Dual career couples have to find creative strategies to prevent role demands and conflicts (p. 199).

In this situation there has to be shared roles and collective child-rearing responsibility (Haralambos and Holborn, 1995). The wife or the husband is not sole provider or has sole housework and childrearing responsibilities. The presence of children can negatively affect the quality of the marriage (Pasley and Grecas, 1984). Parents need to learn the appropriate skills to communicate with children at various levels in order to deepen communication. The giving of care and support must be balanced through the parental period in order to be authoritative parents (Balswick and Balswick, 1999). It is also important to note that research confirmed that the adolescence period is the most difficult parenting period because of issues of independence and control (Pasley and Grecas, 1984). It is also important for parents to have knowledge of what is considered "normal" behavior of children at the various stages of development to lessen the stress and enable them to respond appropriately.

From a sociological perspective, there are new trends that are affecting marriages both positively and negatively. The way that the previous generations related to each other in marriage, given the patriarchal legacy, cannot work in this generation. Women have become more liberated and are standing up for their rights and pressing for their privileges.

Given the social mobility of women, there is the new trend of delaying childbearing until later as women are prepared to put their career before children. This is unique but not without undue pressure. With the birth of a child, if the woman decides to stay home for a while, there can be significant loss in salary that can put significant pressure on the family income and projected plans. There is also the possibility for conflict to develop over how many children to have and when to have them.

A woman going back to college after childbearing, in pursuit of a higher qualification and a better paying job, is also a factor to consider. With the woman studying and working, she has less time for family responsibilities. In addition, the continuous education of partners through distance learning should be carefully handled. It is possible for partners to be at home but too busy for the children and each other. Furthermore, there is the widening of the education gap between men and women in some countries. There is therefore a challenge for some persons to find compatible partners, and so it is highly possible in this kind of context for persons to end up making a poor choice in mate selection.

Finally, from a psychological perspective, in addition to the psychological tasks of marriage discussed earlier, one needs to be sensitive to the psychological impact of the season that a marriage partner is going through. I have come to recognize that marriage has four important seasons based on how normative and non-normative influences affect each partner as explained earlier. These seasons must be properly understood in order to prevent conflict and focus on what is important to one's partner. If one is going through a season and probably thinks that one's partner is going through the same season when this is not so, one could become frustrated. If one does not know the season that one's partner is going through, one will direct one's attention in the wrong direction. Partners do not necessarily go through the same seasons at the same time. Figure 6 gives a presentation of the four seasons:

The first season is inspection, during which a partner is focused on understanding what is going on in the relationship. The other partner is focused on feelings in the relationship and includes examining needs and analyzing areas of intimacy. The analysis is triggered by an emotionally low period in the relationship or just the automatic maintenance principle, which seeks to ensure that one is caring for one's partner's total well-being. It is a search for acceptance and the need to accept one's partner.

The Four Marital Seasons

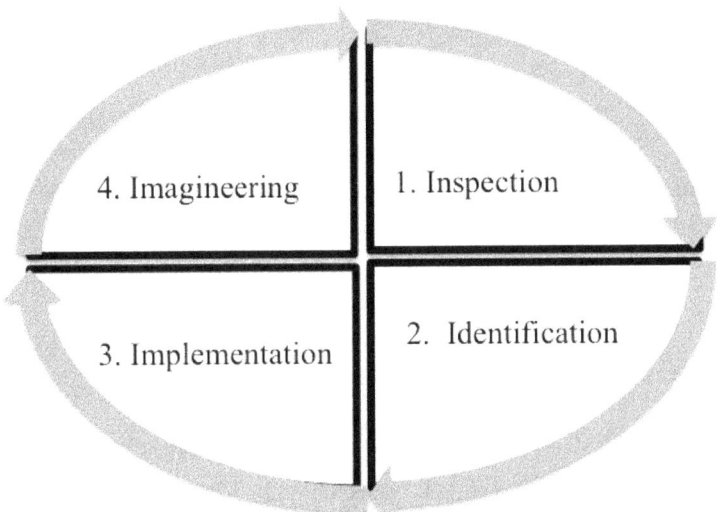

Figure 6

The second season is identification, where a partner is seeking to determine what to focus on such as career, children, projects, parents, community service or more time with partner. It may include joint direct involvement or the specific pursuit of one partner and can be a very rough period. However, setting the three levels of goals (short, medium and long) early in the relationship will help a person to deal with this more effectively.

The third season is implementation and includes attempting to fulfill what one has decided on. There is the need for encouragement, empowerment and empathy in a commitment to support one's partner in reaching the goal. A person should be alert to a partner's need for support when goals sometimes require a lifetime for full implementation.

The final stage is imagineering during which one is looking at the past in celebration or disappointment and projecting for the future with anxiety or hope. One should be aware of how one's partner is viewing the past and the future which will enable one to offer the appropriate support. One should be sensitive to the need for affirmation or assurance.

The cycle is continuous throughout marriage with an emphasis on various aspects of the cycle at different times. Triggered by stagnation as well as change, life circumstances can give a person a good idea of the season that her or his partner is going through. However, the most important factor is one's ability to hear one's partner's concern based on questions asked or comments made.

When a person hears her or his partner's concern, it is important to give full attention to what is being said. Covey (1989, 2004) notes that in order to be effective in interpersonal relationships a person should seek to understand before seeking to be understood. An individual should never respond before really hearing what was actually said. One should say what he or she hears even if he or she does not think he or she heard properly instead of asking his or her partner to repeat. When one says what one has heard, one's partner may have the opportunity to clarify and to take the time to process concerns with an accepting attitude.

INVEST TIME IN LEARNING ABOUT YOUR RELATIONSHIP AND YOUR PARTNER

It takes a number of years to prepare to become a medical doctor or general practitioner and it takes even longer to be a specialist in one of the various subfields in medicine. It is so demanding academically that one needs a solid educational foundation before admission to medical school. Some persons will study at the baccalaureate level to strengthen the academic foundation in order to be admitted into a university to pursue training in medicine. The gatekeepers of the profession will want to ensure academic competence and deter anyone who will potentially be harmful to the public.

The necessity for academic training is true for all occupations which will have more extensive training in some professions. This is not without good reason because a minor gaffe in some professions may be fatal. It has been argued that education makes one trainable and training makes one employable. In any area of life in which one wants to succeed, it is necessary for one to be educated and get the necessary training. The concept of the art and science of various careers suggests that there are principles to be learned and skills to be mastered in doing an effective and efficient job.

It has been noticed that people spend a lot of time learning about anything that they are seriously preparing to master. Marriage, like some professions, can result in personal hurt and harm to others if the principles are not known and properly applied. There is no formal academic training for persons entering marriage. There is no test of competence, so it is the responsibility of those entering to prepare themselves through the reading of materials on the subject and speaking with professionals in the field. Marriage does not need to be a trial and error engagement. Many good books have been written on the subject of understanding and improving one's relationship. If a person is really serious about marriage, active learning is necessary by reading good books or talking to couples with excellent marriages, getting counseling, and so on.

Priority is given to what is important to an individual and one tends to give a lot of attention to learning about career, entertainment and socialization. In comparison to the career paradigm, one should dedicate time in learning about relationship involving one's partner. The lifetime commitment of marital partners suggests that time should be invested in learning about marriage by applying the principles of lifelong learning to improve for enrichment. One only needs to improve his or her investment in marriage by learning how to make it work better.

Product thinking will continuously generate the drive for a person to learn about relationship with a partner. Remember that as an individual learns about relationship and one's partner, one is learning about one's self. This continuous commitment to learn about one's partner and the relationship will cause the development of automaticity which could lead to a flourishing relationship. It is important for an individual to have the right attitude and to learn from others because "iron sharpens iron, but it depends on how they are rubbed together."

The lesson of learning about marriage through the reading of good materials on the subject paid great dividends in my own marriage. Before I got married, I learned that many marriages ended from the honeymoon, based on the approach to sex, especially when the wife or both partners are inexperienced. I internalized this information and acted lovingly towards my partner, given the fact that both of us had no experience. It took some time for us to adjust sexually, but I was aware of what was going on. Our sexual intimacy continues to grow from strength to strength. I was informed through reading, which gave me the ammunition I needed to adjust carefully in our sexual relationship.

The necessity of spending time to learn as much as possible about one's interests, struck me one day when I met an 11-year-old boy on the beach. This youngster knew a lot about swimming, the ocean and sea life. He said that he spent a lot of time reading in this area, because he wants to become a marine biologist. He told me that when others are afraid of going to the sea in a storm, he is not afraid because he knows what to do. In no way did I get the impression that he was putting his life at risk.

Then and there I thought to myself that I really wanted to be a good swimmer, but I have never really read anything about swimming. I was forced to consider other subject areas in which I may need to do some reading. I also acknowledged that when a person thinks something can be learned naturally, he or she tends not to invest time in learning properly. This summed up my attitude towards swimming.

An individual can build a successful marriage by taking time to learn the art and science of marriage and not leave success to chance. A person should give one's self a better chance at succeeding more rapidly by learning from others. Carson (1992) corroborates my assertion in his claim that "reading is the way out of ignorance, and the road to achievement" (p. 17). Ignorance can kill a good thing and thus the claim is applicable to marriage as an individual needs to become positively addicted to reading to enhance a marital relationship and life in general.

The best way to get to know someone is to spend both quality and quantity time with the person. One will get to know a lot through conversations. Asking direct questions and opinions will cause a person to discover a lot as well. However, just observing the relationships of one's partner and social involvement can be a good window through which one can learn a great deal about a partner.

Situation Related Questions

An individual can ensure that a successful marriage is built on the basis of product thinking and egalitarianism only based on the right attitude. One has to get rid of cancerous activities in order to develop the right attitude. Green (2006) uses the concept and analogy of the cancerous mind, feet, hands, ears, eyes and heart to show how powerful negative thoughts and beliefs are and the resulting negative impacts of cancerous activities. The starting point in building an egalitarian marriage guided by product thinking, is fixing one's attitude. Attitude in this regard has to do with an evaluation of a partner and a person's thoughts, feelings and actions, in relation to the loved one. One needs to develop a positive attitude, not a negative or neutral attitude—if one has issues, counseling is an alternative to work through these problems. The willingness to seek counseling if needed is a very good move in developing the right attitude and taking responsibility. When one reflects on the metaphors for marriage, which are positive and objectively chosen, the reflection will generate the kind of product thinking that will radically change his or her attitude for the betterment of a marital relationship. Product thinking, leading to automaticity, can be developed by learning to ask the right questions in relation to one's partner.

There is a tendency for human beings to be self-centered, as persons are always thinking about their needs and seeking ways and means of fulfilling them. In marriage, it has been argued that there are two need systems. Harley (1997) proposes that the five basic emotional needs of man are sexual fulfillment, recreational companionship, an attractive spouse, domestic support and admiration. Harley (1997) further argues that the five basic emotional needs of a woman are affection, conversation, honesty and openness, financial support and family commitment. The author notes too, that the categories identified may not equally apply to all but the inevitable conclusion suggests that the emotional needs of men and women are different. Therefore, men and women should not make the assumption that their needs are similar to those of their marital partners.

Others have proposed that some needs are more important than others. According to the proponents of this view, needs are to be met according to those that are considered more important. Gray (1992) posits the view that the primary love needs of women are caring, understanding, respect, devotion, validation and reassurance. In contrast, the primary love needs of men are trust, acceptance, appreciation, admiration, approval and encouragement. Gray (1992) further argues that the primary love needs of men and women are similar and both genders need to receive all twelve, the primary needs first in order for the secondary needs to be appreciated.

Although I agree that there are needs that each partner has in marriage, I also believe that because this phenomenon is guided by sum thinking, there is a tendency to focus on one's self in terms of seeking the fulfillment of personal needs, which is destructive to the relationship. Therefore product thinking argues for reciprocity of emotional needs in an egalitarian relationship. It is not about fulfilling needs because needs are met by serving a partner out of love yet understanding how a partner wants to receive love is very important as an individual needs to understand a partner and serves out of that understanding.

If a person speaks a language that a partner cannot understand then that person will not be heard by a partner. It is very important for a person to know how a partner wants to be treated before an attempt to do so as love perceived is love received. A person needs to discover the language that a partner wants him or her to speak and speak it. If one does not know the language, one spends the time to learn it. It is possible to discover a partner's most important love language and learn to speak it. Chapman (2004) states that the five love languages are words of affirmation, quality time, receiving gifts, acts of service, and physical touch. One needs to discover one's partner's primary love language(s) and speak it.

It is important for a person to move away from seeking the fulfillment of his or her own need to serving his or her partner. This means that even if a person thinks that one's needs are not being met, there will be ways and means of serving a partner's best interest. Genuine love is not motivated by mere reciprocity but heart and mind commitment. There is a tendency for a spouse to stop looking out for a partner's best interest when there is the perception that personal interests are not taken into consideration.

Love is about having the courage to serve when one would rather be served; having the wisdom to forget about self and focus on one's spouse. It is by ensuring that a compassionate heart is cultivated towards a partner that makes an individual forget about reciprocity and serves selflessly.

I have found that it is important to ask myself situational related questions even when I feel that some of my "own" needs are not being met. For example, I ask myself "What would I want my partner to do for me if I was in this situation that my partner is in now?" In this way I can make a concerted effort to enter into my partner's world. It is this heartfelt compassion that fuels my desire to serve my partner in the midst of not being served as I desire to be served. In order to succeed in doing this, one has to try to imagine what one's partner is feeling and bring the self into that emotional experience. A person should make a commitment to "always be with" her or his partner, constantly tuning into one's partner's emotions.

It might be difficult (at times) to imagine what a partner is feeling if that feeling is not shared by a partner. However, a spouse can respond gently to spark warmth and openness as well as give time and space where necessary. One should avoid unnecessary words when things seem challenging by being quick to listen and slow to speak. One's speech should motivate, encourage, support and ameliorate the negative impact even when dealing with the most sensitive issues. The spoken words must be like salt, preserve by preventing things from getting worse and enhance by adding flavor.

A New Relational Paradigm

When things are not going according to expectations a person should not allow words to not go according to the expectations of a partner. "Remember that whatever went wrong has gone bad already" therefore do not make what is bad worse. I am in concert with Wheat's (1983) assertion that one should "consistently show ... [one's] mate respect and honor commanded in Scripture whether ... [one's] mate personally merits it or not" (p. 31). Look for lessons, not necessarily answers. When one looks for lessons there must be an ability to learn them without pushing or pressuring a partner. The direct involvement of a spouse will not be needed to learn the lessons from situations that confront him or her.

Looking for lessons is a new paradigm for maintaining healthy relationships by seeking for lessons to be learned and not for answers that will cause a person to avoid a lot of negative feedback in a relationship. One should learn about one's partner every day and become a lifelong learner not a lifelong complainer. Instead of asking a partner, why did you do this? an individual can ask what can I learn from this? Applying this rule can allow a person to operate with an attitude that suggests that a partner's motives are fair.

One should always think the best of his or her partner regardless of the situation and make a commitment to always think positively about the other person. This sounds like the very important "trust factor" which strengthens a marriage to become impermeable to negative attitudes. Negative attitudes will weaken trust and security in a marriage and expose the relationship to the venom of doubt and fear. The faces and dynamics of fear prevent security and create an impossible environment for relaxation. Benner (2003) notes that anxiety can be so crippling that it makes commitment to love impossible (p. 44). Tensions will be created in a relationship where the partners are not relaxed.

Fundamentals of Situational Questions

The situational questions that warrant asking in seeking to serve a partner's best interest must be rooted in areas in which human beings want love to be communicated to them. There are certain ways in which people appreciate expressions of love. For example, a person needs to know the ways in which a partner prefers to be treated. If one responds "inappropriately" there could be a misunderstanding resulting in a further distancing instead of reopening the lines of communication in the relationship. A spouse's affirmation of a partner when the partner just wants to be listened to may result in further emotional pain. The following are some situational questions that could be asked in relation to a spouse:

1) Would I want my partner to affirm me?

A spouse needs to listen to his or her partner actively by being completely tuned in to his or her partner. A spouse should be with his or her partner completely and not just listen for words only but to the level of emotional intensity and non-verbal behaviors.

Having heard a partner's cry, a person can assess whether the partner wants to be affirmed by reminding the partner of his or her strengths. Love for the partner may need to be restated through a love letter of appreciation.

An individual can cultivate the habit of being a number one cheerleader and should know when to stop cheering or start cheering. When the world appears to be against one's spouse, a shoulder of comfort and cheer should be provided as an oasis in times of stress and tension.

2) Would I want my partner to forgive me?

An individual needs to be careful about spending unnecessary time arguing about the offering of forgiveness. Sometimes all a partner needs to hear is, 'I forgive you'. A partner does not need condemnation but an expression of forgiveness which is further demonstrated in the attitude.

It is very important for a spouse to know that if his or her partner does not hear him or her say that he or she has forgiven him or her it can lead to further disengagement. If a spouse does not say that he or she has forgiven the partner then it is hard for the partner to know what is in the spouse's heart. Saying that one is forgiven is different from hearing and accepting an apology. Saying that one is forgiven is a way of totally releasing one's partner.

3) Would I want my partner to listen to me?

The issue of listening is a challenge for many people as some persons do not know how to really listen. An individual has to learn how to listen to a partner by spending some time learning effective communication skills or listening skills. One needs to listen to the other partner so that a partner can feel that his or her counterpart is really listening in order to feel understood. This can only be demonstrated through effective listening skills.

In demonstrating effective listening skills, attention should be paid to a partner's emotions at the emotional level before seeking to respond at the cognitive level. If one partner is feeling hurt, the other person should authenticate the hurt by acknowledging it before offering any explanation. One needs to respond at the appropriate level to stimulate positive emotion and to enhance communication.

4) Would I want my partner to give me some space?

Proper timing is vital in every undertaking in life. If one's timing is poor, it can be explained by the cultural more, "bad luck is worse than necromancy" ("conjuration of the spirits of the dead for purposes of magically revealing the future or influencing the course of events - Necromancy, 2008)" or being perplexed by unexplainable forces. It is therefore in one's best interest to assess the situation before pushing the "button" due to a partner needing a little space to work through emotions being experienced.

Life is filled with problems and sometimes a person cannot even imagine what his or her partner may be going through. Providing space with a caring attitude might make the situation better by demonstrating in a caring way. For example, 'it seems as if I have hurt you and I am still making the situation worse, I think I need a little time to reflect'. Taking time and initiative to reflect will also give one's partner some space for the spouse to use this time to write the partner a love letter. This will be a powerful tool of communication because the partner will realize that his or her spouse was still thinking about him or her while on timeout.

5) Would I want my partner to be frank with me?

There are times when a person is going through a challenging period and would love to hear an honest response from a partner. A spouse who has the tendency to say things to prevent a partner from feeling worse without being honest will be least helpful. Healing takes place when the truth is spoken in love, and though there is the potential to create further hurt, it can lead to better healing.

It is important for a spouse to be frank, when the situation warrants, timing is critical so that a frank remark can be properly internalized especially when it is negative. A frank response is based on a spouse's commitment to devotion in every way to the relationship by empowering her or his partner to become the best.

A spouse should learn when to say what the partner needs to hear and not what she or he thinks a partner wants to hear. In areas where a spouse needs to be developed in his or her profession, a partner can be the greatest critic and spur excellence. There has to be trust in a relationship for this to be effective.

6) Would I want my partner to spend some time with me?

Sometimes when a spouse is going through the problems of life the spouse will immediately need a partner to spend some time with him or her. The time being spent should be focused completely on a partner's interests by not calling the "shots" for any engagement or encounter as the quality time spent should be on the partner's terms. Finally, spending time with a partner is a powerful demonstration of love.

GIVE THANKS FOR YOUR PARTNER

A spouse should not forget a partner's past kindness as learning to give thanks will provide a reason to care. Thanksgiving will have a powerful effect on one's heart since a transforming power is in thanksgiving as it generates hope. When an attitude of thanksgiving is developed a person will have to take note of the positives, which is essential in product thinking.

It is important for a spouse to learn to give thanks as a part of the product thinking paradigm because a person sees a partner's faults clearly and more easily than one's own. Whenever one focuses on the negatives in any area of life, the positives are dwarfed and when one comes to focus on the positives, the negatives are dwarfed. As a result, negative little things can become big things and a person ends up "sweating the small stuff."

An individual needs to give thanks for a partner by focusing on strengths and areas where support can be provided in the following segments of living, the economic, family, spiritual, social, emotional, psychological, mental, physical, occupational, sexual, marital, communication, the purpose-driven, areas of intimacy and the parental. For example, if a spouse is doing well in any of these areas that is a strength in the relationship and it should be celebrated. Narramore (1960) affirms the importance of this in his observation that "counsellors help marriage partners to look for and appreciate strengths in their mates" (p. 192). This affirmation is based on the fact that many marital problems stem from lack of appreciation, which begins to be demonstrated in words and deeds. Wheat and Wheat (1997) state that another aspect of loving a partner involves thanking God for every good quality in a partner as people often complain about the undesirable qualities and overlook the qualities that originally attracted them (p. 37).

A marriage partner should constantly look for things to give thanks for and to celebrate in the relationship. People tend to feel connected to individuals who highlight their strengths not those who are constantly talking about their weaknesses (Feldman, 2005). A spouse should make his or her appreciation known verbally and to seek to comb through the relationship by examining areas in which some thanks can be given as this is indispensable to build a lifelong relationship. Giving thanks can impact the emotions positively through the realization that a lot of good things are going on for a person which could cause celebration with one's spouse. Marital reflection weakens marital frustration as well as enhances marital stamina.

A spouse should therefore make a commitment to always focus on the positives. Thoughts affect feelings and actions are important from a cognitive behavioral perspective (Dobson, 2001; Jones and Butman, 1991). It is the plan of the "enemy," due to human brokenness and bondage, to dupe one into focusing on the negatives. The enemy wants a person to distort the picture by targeting feelings and behaviors in order to create negative feelings in an attempt to destroy one's marriage. One should not allow the enemy to stir up negative feelings in him or her when there is a lot to be positive about.

One should always give thanks for that which is worth having as a marriage is worth protecting or rescuing; one should give thanks for a partner. A couple is the product of their union and should view the marital union as joining together for life. Give thanks for this union that has been established and celebrate its existence with anticipation of ultimate fulfillment. A marital partner ought to give thanks that he or she is a part of the union which celebrates and rekindles intimacy, sparks passion and regenerates commitment. An individual can give thanks that he or she has been given the opportunity to love someone by giving him or her an opportunity to grow and mature.

12

Marshalling Marital Skills

THE CHALLENGES THAT PEOPLE face today are complex and at times very frustrating. Suffering in a marital relationship is not necessarily because a couple is deliberately doing things to negatively affect the relationship. It is due to being too busy, tired, frustrated, and emotionally drained to consciously notice that the relationship is being negatively affected. The irony, however, is that one does not have to deliberately do things to cause one's marriage to fail, but one has to deliberately prevent her or his marriage from the wear and tear of life that may result in stress and subsequent marital failure.

Life is filled with changes, challenges, crises, consequences and conflicts. A commitment to a marital relationship is important to develop coping strategies in order to avoid conflicts, relate properly to others, adjust to changes, turn challenges into opportunities, and avoid negative consequences. Commitment to marriage will motivate an individual to make adequate preparation in order to discover and fulfill one's purpose(s). The following are some important areas that warrant attention in order to prevent a marriage from imploding and engender marital satisfaction.

COMMUNICATION

Normal family functioning includes effective communication between members (Nichols, 2004). Communication is the channel of relationship in the form of giving, sharing, caring, and affirming. Nichols (2004) maintains that "although conflict doesn't magically disappear when family members start to listen to each other, it's unlikely that conflicts will get solved before people start to listen to each other (Nichols, 1995)" (p. 76).

Most persons are not motivated to listen to others until they feel heard and understood.

Although communication is something that a person does naturally, it is a very complex process. Lack of awareness of this process will facilitate the distortions that are inherent in communication. Given the complexity of communication, a number of models have been developed to explain the process. At the basic level, communication involves the sending and receiving of messages. Baran (2004) notes that "in its simplest form communication is the transmission of a message from a source to a receiver" (p. 4). Additionally, for effective communication to take place it involves a sender encoding a message and a receiver decoding that message and giving feedback.

There are several components to communication. Adler and Elmhorst (2005) note that these include: sender, message, encoding, channel, receiver, decoding, feedback, and noise. Noise is used here in both the psychological as well as the physical sense. The complex nature of communication makes it difficult to completely illustrate the process. There are some aspects that cannot be represented in a diagram. Adler and Elmhorst (2005) being aware of the limitations in illustrating the communication process give a useful synecdoche in a process where both communicators send and receive as they encode or decode messages through whatever channel(s) chosen. Furthermore, this interactive communication process is affected by various kinds of "noise" to include environmental and psychological. Notwithstanding, a more basic model of the communication process may be delineated as shown in the synecdoche, illustrated in Figure 7. In this basic model, the process commences when the sender encodes a message, which is then sent through a channel. The message is decoded by the receiver who then encodes a message. This message is then sent as a feedback through a channel so that when the sender gets the feedback, it is decoded. If after the sender decodes the message, it conveys what the individual had intended to communicate, the process is completed. In effective communication, this process continues with changes in who the sender and receiver are, so that at times, the sender is the receiver and the receiver is the sender.

A Basic Model of the Communication Process

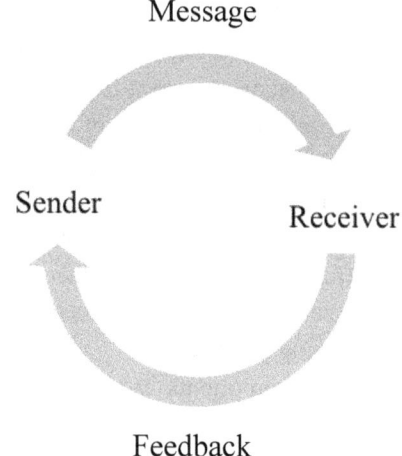

Figure 7

There are three ways of communicating: one-way, two-way, and interactive or transactional. One-way communication involves the mere giving of information. Two-way communication involves giving feedback. Interactive communication involves feedback but includes the processing of information at the deeper level, including attention to emotions, nonverbal cues, and sensitivity to barriers in the communication process. In interactive communication, feelings are reflected and an attempt is made to ensure that the message is clearly understood.

There are many barriers to communication, one of which is sometimes referred to as noise. These barriers are both internal and external in that the former has to do with factors inside the sender and the receiver. These factors include egotism, defensiveness, hostility, perfectionism, fear, and low self-esteem. The external factors are those issues that the sender or the receiver has no direct control over that distort the message as environmental noise.

There are two basic levels involved in communication: report and command (Nichols, 2004). Report has to do with the information that is passed on while command has to do with how the receiver is expected to act. The message in this process contains both facts and emotions. To put it another way, the levels of communication involve content and relationship messages, which are related to affinity, control and respect (Adler and Elmhorst, 2005).

Family members are able to communicate feelings freely and openly with each other out of a mature personhood as it is contingent upon trust and commitment (Balswick and Balswick, 1999, p. 32). A failure in communication can result in a form of paradoxical communication where one person encourages the other to talk freely about emotions and then feel hurt when the person is honest and open (Nichols, 2004).

Research has shown that effective communication and problem solving skills are important in resolving conflicts. An individual needs to be aware of the styles of communication in order to improve problem solving and conflict resolution skills. A form of communication style includes summarization, reflective listening, and restatement (Corey, 2000, p. 299). Another is called the speaker-listener technique, which includes one person speaking while the other listens without interruptions (Jordan, Stanley, and Markman, 1999, p. 28). If these two styles are properly implemented, there are great dividends in addition to the expected result of a relationship in which issues are carefully handled.

Self-disclosure is important in intimate relationships (Myers, 2005). The level at which persons communicate indicate how much they are prepared to disclose. There are five levels of communication identified by some theorists. The five levels are small talk, factual conversation, ideas and opinion, feelings and emotions, and deep insight (Pelt, 1997, p. 64).

The need for proper communication is indispensable to proper interpersonal relationships. One's ability to connect with persons in significant ways allows for common understanding. Effective communication is even more important in marriage because it is often intimate and intense. There is the temptation to become too relaxed when communicating with a partner because of the tendency to believe that a partner knows and understands and therefore one does not have to say everything. This is a dangerous misconception in light of the fact that an enemy to effective communication is mind reading. It is important for one to speak clearly so that one's partner does not have to make assumptions.

Although there are many theories on effective communication the principles of communication are applicable even to the marital relationship. There needs to be a process for communicating in marriage which has specific stages of consistency for a person seeking to deal with situations, circumstances or issues. Figure 8 gives a presentation and explanation of a new conceptualization of the marital communication process.

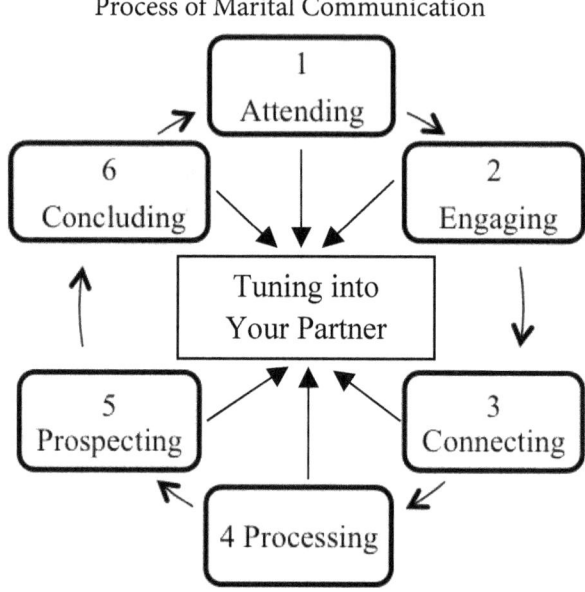

Figure 8

The six processes of communication in marriage indicate that there are six important things for one to do in deliberately tuning into one's partner. Tuning in refers to "being with" and attempting to completely understand one's partner and demonstrating that understanding in one's response and support. Response has to do with communicating that one understands, and support has to do with demonstrating that one understands.

Attending

The first process is attending. When one's partner is communicating with a partner it is very important for the individual to attend to what a partner is saying. A spouse should face his or her partner and maintain eye contact by paying complete attention by not allowing his or her mind to focus on other things or thinking. A spouse will not know if the attending process is effective until he or she has completely heard the comments again. Note that when a spouse is saying something again, it could very well be that one did not respond appropriately the first time when the comment was made or there is some new development based on previous dialogue on the matter.

A spouse should learn to allow his or her partner to speak directly by directly facing the person. When one partner speaks and the other is not facing his or her partner, words can be easily distorted. Pay attention to words, body language and tone when communicating and if one is unable to engage in a conversation at a given time, this should be communicated carefully.

Engaging

The second process is engaging. One should never allow a partner to feel like he or she is the only one involved in the communication process. A spouse needs to engage the other party with attention and behaviors by effective body language and exclamatory remarks to encourage the partner to keep talking or clarify where necessary. It is very important for a spouse to be genuine. Be very careful and ensure that the wrong attending behaviors are not used at inappropriate places (one should not say yes! when one should have said oh no!). One should also ask questions in a way that suggests that he or she is seeking information and not checking motive. For example, instead of questioning the lateness of one's spouse one could find out what happened to cause the lateness. The question of Why puts one's partner on the defensive and could cause one's partner to stop talking or respond inappropriately.

Connecting

The third process is connecting and one should learn to connect with a partner at the feeling level. Given what a spouse has shared to his or her partner the individual should ensure that appropriate words are used to describe an understanding of his or her partner's feelings. Validate a spouse's feelings. Don't make the mistake of saying that he or she should not be feeling like that. Never ignore the emotion but instead seek to communicate an understanding of the intensity or level of the emotion. For example, if one's partner was unfairly treated and came home crying the other party would not say that "I can see that you were hurt by the situation". Instead the other party would say, "I can see that you are deeply hurt as you were unfairly treated by someone who should have known better". One of the keys to open doors into the heart of a partner is the ability to let him or her feel understood.

Processing

The fourth is processing where the information is processed at the cognitive level. This is where an individual seeks for clarification and for information. Do not provide an opinion, but try to see the partner's viewpoints by processing the issue from various perspectives for insights and clarity. An individual should pay attention to non-verbal communication and be aware of the process of effective communication discussed earlier. One should also engage one's partner in looking at the issue from various perspectives.

Prospecting

The fifth process is called prospecting where provision of support should be made for a spouse. An individual might encourage, challenge, uphold, rebuke or affirm one's partner. Through all of this, a spouse's objective is to give hope through being able to disagree and still give hope. For example, if one disagrees with a partner's decision to buy something one could say, "Honey, I know that you make good decisions and that you take my comments seriously that's why you are discussing this with me. However, on this occasion I do not believe that you are making a wise choice." As a spouse, one needs to avoid surface communication like merely saying ok, good, all right, I don't know, I have nothing to say, you make me feel, and so on. Couples should avoid cursory communication and seek to defer communication if the timing is not appropriate as a spouse should not be taciturn in marital communication.

Concluding

The final process of communication is concluding where a common understanding is reached after responding and supporting. Couples should state their positions clearly to each other. Both partners may decide to follow-up with each other at a later date or after completing assigned tasks within this communication domain.

The process of communication might sound like hard work but the principles are not difficult to apply. They can be applied to a greater or lesser extent in one's interactions as partners. A spouse should allow for a response to the other party's feeling before engaging in discussion on the issue or concern. When a couple is aware of what should be involved in the communication process, the appropriate response and support will be provided. Beyond the process of tuning into a partner, a system needs developing for keeping informed. A spouse could apply strategies, such as sharing schedules; e-mailing relevant information the moment they come to one's attention; sharing a diary; installing a bulletin board at home; and sending delayed messages by the use of technology. The individual should also send the message to himself or herself so that he or she is reminded the moment the message is sent.

CONFLICT MANAGEMENT

It was mentioned that conflict is a part of healthy relationships. In light of this reality, one needs to learn how to deal with conflict in order to lessen the negative impact on a relationship. An individual needs to learn how to deal with conflict appropriately to be assured of a healthy relationship. At the heart of dealing with conflict effectively is the commitment to be a peacemaker. When a conflict develops, an attitude should be guided by the principles of being quick to listen, slow to speak and slow to become angry. This must also be guided by a willingness to forgive the other spouse in order to reduce conflict.

Knowing how conflicts develop is just as crucial as knowing how to manage conflict. Many theories on conflict management are available and are very useful but there is the need to paint a vivid picture of conflict development to effectively manage it in the marriage relationship.

Figure 9 represents a graphic presentation of how conflict develops and escalates. A conflict is set in motion when an unpleasant situation occurs or is threatening. The environmental stimulus develops into a conflict when the person starts to think negatively about the situation. The negative cognitive reaction causes negative emotions to arise. The situation sets one's mental processes in motion that automatically produce the emotions. The emotions usually include fear, regret, disappointment, anger, and disgust.

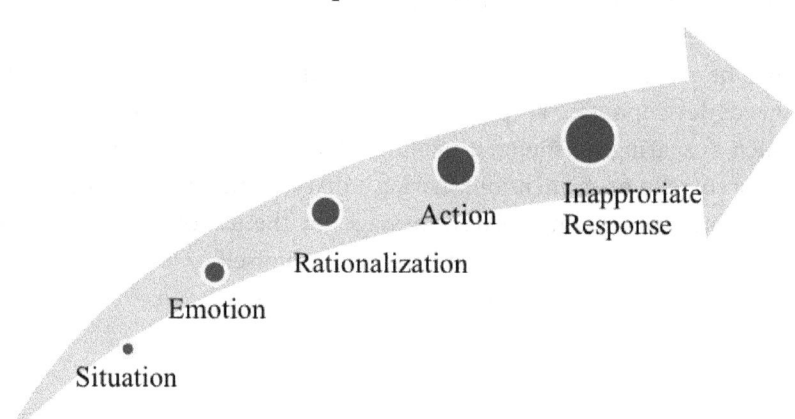

Figure 9

It is normal for some persons to act immediately on the basis of their emotions. However, it is better for persons to take time out to think through the situation as they probably justify their perspective and this intensifies the emotion. Whenever the emotion is weakened by rationalization, a person's actions are more likely to be mild. The approach adapted in dealing with the situation lies more in seeking clarity than casting blame; it is more relational than confrontational.

If the person being confronted responds with negative feedback, it intensifies the conflict within the relationship. In addition, if the party who is being affected perceives that the other party is taking him or her for granted, conflict is intensified. The reaction of the person receiving information can strengthen the conflict through an inappropriate response, which is at the root of a conflict escalating. However, couples can prevent that conflict from escalating in their relationship as product thinking allows a partner to think win-win at all times.

Management of Self in Relation to Conflict

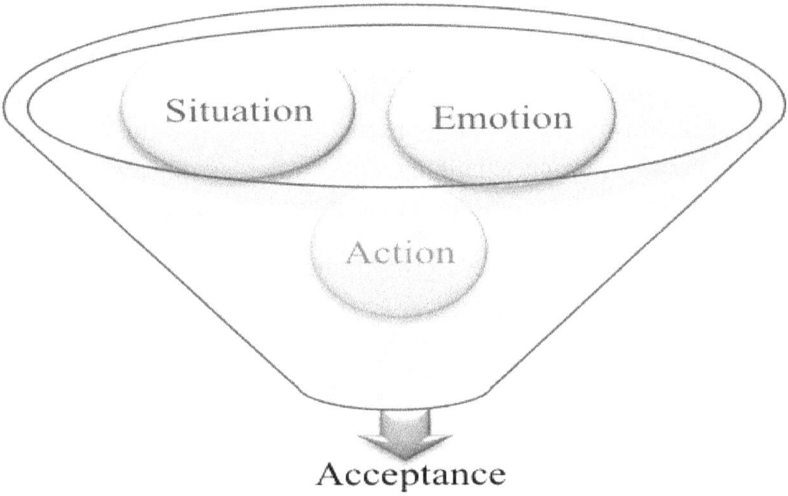

Situation **Emotion**

Action

↓

Acceptance

Figure 10

Figure 10 presents an illustration of how conflict can be prevented from escalating. The diagram shows how the appropriate response can prevent the escalation of conflicts by affirming a partner's emotions. Don't move to agree or disagree or even process the situation before responding positively to the emotions of one's partner. A spouse wants to know that his or her partner is imagining how he or she is feeling. Although one may not agree with the way one's partner is feeling; it is the feeling of one's partner which needs an affirmation.

After one works through the emotions by identifying and affirming his or her partner's feelings, one can now begin to talk about the situation through listening to the account of the situation and then to provide an appropriate response. Make sure to focus on the situation at hand; do not drift off into other situations but focus on the issue and avoid distractions that can build unnecessary tension.

After processing the situation by objectively talking it over, forgiveness should be sought if one was wrong in one's perception. One should also ask for forgiveness if one caused hurt or pain to a spouse. Never apologize and give excuses, as a person would have already processed the situation to know the ins and outs of the situation. One should accept forgiveness and offer forgiveness through an objective to accept each other not reject each other. Marriages end in conflict because persons are unwilling to forgive, which causes them to be angry and thus prevents them from being able to amicably work through issues.

AUTHENTIC LOVE

It is only a willingness to love authentically that is going to make the big difference in a marriage. One has to be prepared to love regardless and in spite of. This kind of love is motivated by the right attitude, which is indispensable to product thinking. Look at the big difference that attitude can make as presented in the equations in figure 11.

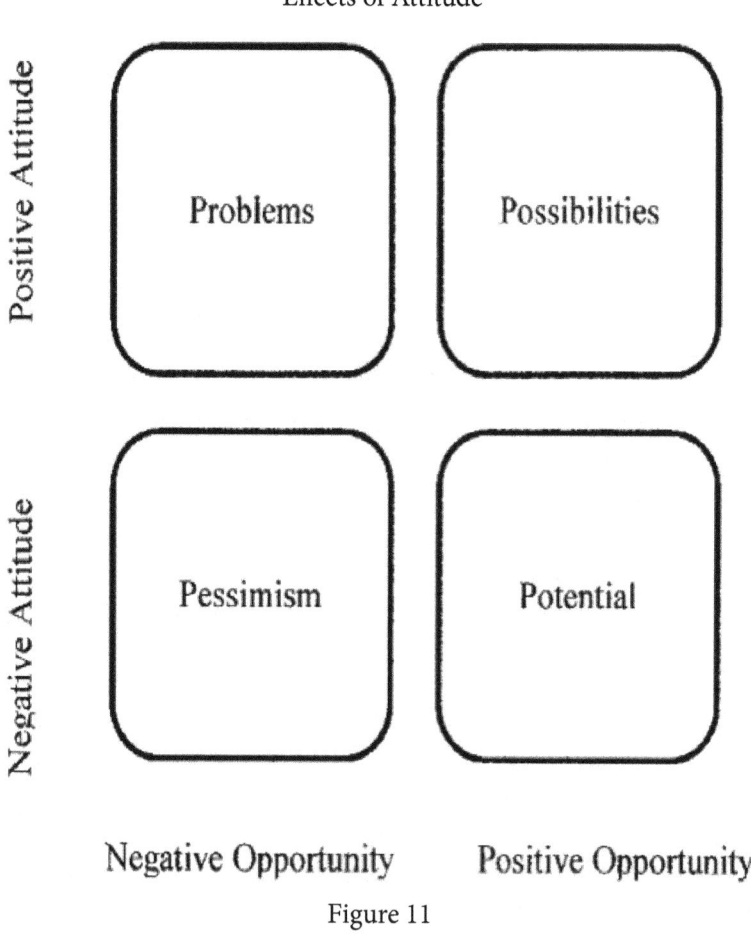

Figure 11

In a marriage, if a spouse has a negative attitude and there are favorable circumstances there will be problems. If a spouse has a negative attitude and there are unfavorable circumstances there is going to be pessimism, which is destructive to the health of a relationship that should be purpose-driven. A positive attitude, even if the circumstances are unfavorable, will result in great potential. With the right attitude one can change obstacles into opportunities by being positive in response to the circumstances that are favorable. There are even greater productive possibilities. When the right attitude meets potential, the future is amazingly bright. Authentic love has to be built on a positive attitude made possible through product thinking.

In order to know if one loves authentically, it is good to have a graphic presentation of authentic love as measured against one's love for a partner. The question surrounds what authentic love looks like in a marriage. Authentic love must bring together all the components and dimensions of love which have been discussed in the Marital Love Cycle and the Johari Window of Love. Love requires an expression and authentic love requires continuous expression both in words and deeds.

Intimacy

Figure 12 presents a graphic representation of authentic love with the four components of intimacy, passion, compassion and commitment. Greeff and Malherbe (2001) have made several observations on the subject of intimacy. Many persons marry to obtain intimacy which is positively correlated with marital satisfaction. Enhancing marital intimacy increases marital satisfaction overtime. Satisfaction with a sexual relationship is linked to the level of family functioning. Intimacy in the other areas of marriage is connected to sexual satisfaction. Men and women appear to differ in their views on intimacy and marital satisfaction. Intimacy plays a different role for men and women. Finally, men use sex to increase intimacy and women need intimacy to become sexually intimate.

Authentic Love

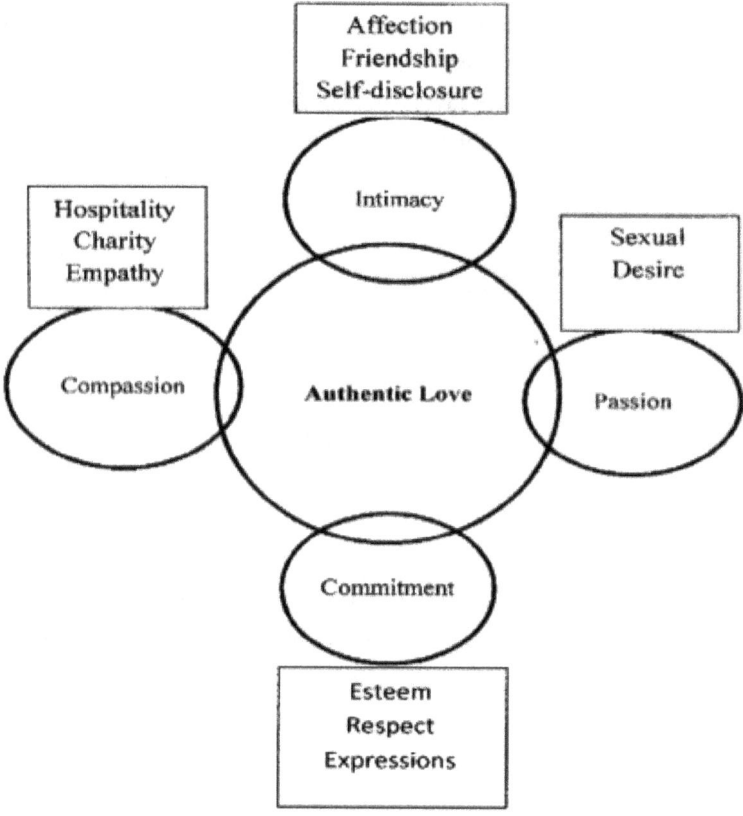

Figure 12

The importance of intimacy in a relationship cannot be overstated. Greeff and Malherbe (2001) in a South African study conclude that:

> Significant differences between men and women were found on two of the five aspects of experienced intimacy [social, emotional, recreational, sexual, and intellectual] (sexual and recreational) as well as for social and sexual discrepancy scores (difference between experienced and desired intimacy). With the exception of social intimacy as experienced by women, a positive correlation was found for both sexes between all the components of experienced intimacy and marital satisfaction. No differences were found for experienced intimacy or marital satisfaction according to family developmental stages. (p. 247)

Although this study was conducted in Africa, it has implications for the Western hemisphere. The study underscores the fact that intimacy is important for marital satisfaction and not predicated on the family developmental stages. Tolsted and Stokes (1983) in a study confirm the role of intimacy in marital satisfaction. The study suggests that some areas of intimacy are more important, in that the level of verbal and affective intimacy made stronger contributions to the prediction of marital satisfaction than the contribution made by physical intimacy (p. 573).

Intimacy in marriage is directly impacted by affection and friendship that is related to level of self-disclosure (Myers, 2005). Affection and friendship are demonstrated in a caring attitude towards one's partner. This high level of caring and sharing will allow intimacy to intensify. The presence of warmth and close connection creates a sense of belonging. A couple therefore continues to spend a lot of time together and to enjoy each other's company. A high level of intimacy will cause a couple to feel comfortable in each other's company.

Friendship is integral to intimacy and it is one of the secrets to building and sustaining intimacy in a marital relationship. Pelt (1997) from a study involving four hundred divorced men, conclude that the marriages fell apart due to a lack of continuation of close friendship with partners. Couples normally consider each other as best friends at the beginning of their marriage. An intimate friendship is important in nurturing a marital relationship. In studies with married couples, they normally put being best friends at the top of the list of things that keep their marriages together (Pelt, 1997).

A relationship continues to grow as intimacy becomes interwoven in each partner's life. Intimacy impacts the mental, social, physical, psychological, emotional and spiritual areas of individuals. Marital intimacy suggests very deep connection between partners involving friendship and affection which involves unselfish caring and sharing with a spouse in the relationship.

The level of intimacy in marriage will impact marital satisfaction where the end result is to get closer and not farther apart by one's attitudes or actions. Many areas of intimacy need reinforcing to keep a relationship alive. Intimacy will lead to need fulfillment and this significantly contributes to marital satisfaction.

The types of intimacy proposed by relationship specialists in the literature are diverse. However, the factors discussed in the following pages are very important in cultivating a fulfilling marriage because a relationship will grow when couples explore the various avenues of intimacy. A marital relationship will never become unexciting when a couple is consciously exploring the channels of intimacy. Couples should deliberately build the areas of intimacy in the marital relationship until it becomes a habit for them to do various intimate things together.

The Anatomy of Intimacy

Intimacy wears many faces due to its intricacy as it pervades every aspect of live. An individual should strive for intimacy in every area of life with a marital partner. These areas of intimacy include:

- Emotional intimacy—sharing of deep feelings and encouraging the other party to do the same.
- Social intimacy—spending time in interaction with others at an event or movie.
- Recreational intimacy—playing together in some activity that requires exertion of energy.
- Spiritual intimacy—sharing one's relationship with the supernatural and the meaning of life.
- Physical intimacy—touching each other; caressing in meaningful ways.
- Psychological intimacy - stimulating each other to process things at a deeper level to allow for healing through proper reflection and relationship.
- Sexual intimacy—the enjoyment of coitus or orgasmic release.
- Intellectual intimacy—sharing knowledge from books or other sources as well as opinions to stimulate the mind.
- Crisis intimacy—working through painful experiences together.
- Common cause intimacy—investing one's time in a project that both partners are passionate about.
- Vocational intimacy—sharing about what is happening in one's job and one's career plans.
- Parenting intimacy—sharing about child-rearing issues or matters relating to one's own parents.

- Household intimacy—sharing in homemaking.
- Aesthetic intimacy—sharing about experiences and enjoying beauty.
- Creative intimacy—sharing in art.
- Conflict intimacy—working through conflicts together to bring about resolution.
- Commitment intimacy—mutual investment of time and proper attitude in maintaining the relationship.
- Communication intimacy—time spent seeking to be understood and seeking to understand one's partner through the use of effective and efficient communication techniques.

Intimacy does not just happen; it has to be created. It is a process that goes on after a conscious investment of time. When it is automatic, doing things together as a couple becomes the norm. The level of intimacy in a relationship is proportionate to the types of intimacy shared. Love will improve through intimacy as the level of intimacy intensifies.

Passion

Passion is very important in marriage and product thinking warrants an individual telling himself or herself that a partner is the best. An individual needs to be turned on by a partner at all times by stimulating the mind and emotions of the other party as love making takes place in an atmosphere where romance is kindled through tenderness of heart. The female should strive to remain physically attractive so that the male will always be turned on by her sexually. Pulchritude on the path of both partners is indispensible to foster sensual pleasure. Both partners should regale each other. A couple should allow for derivation of pleasure from thinking about each other. Taking the time to caress and romance one's partner is important. A couple should strive not to leave or rejoin each other's presence without kissing. Do not let the week pass without massaging! Husbands, be careful that you are not misunderstood by conveying the message that sex is all that is on your mind.

Product thinking is an important position that should be consciously worked on in order to improve the marital relationship. The attitude should be "I am in this for a lifetime so let me make the best of it. I can really work at enjoying my relationship." This should be a motivation to continue empowering one's partner. A spouse should provide encouragement and motivation for a partner to increase a spouse's relationship potential.

A spouse should do everything to build a partner's confidence even in lovemaking by being gracious and kind with the giving of compliments. One should not be fulsome in expressions of praise and commendations but seek to be creative by writing poems or songs, weekly dates, reflecting on past experiences, projects and sharing as expressions of love.

Commitment

A spouse's commitment should cause him or her to be careful in the use of words, actions, spending money, lovemaking, child-rearing, humor, speech and general conduct. An individual's commitment fosters the necessity of compromising as the need arises. The need to compromise causes one to be committed in building an egalitarian relationship.

A spouse's commitment causes communication to be deliberate and searching for something to celebrate by making a big thing out of a partner's accomplishments, special days or occasions. Commitment engenders co-vision in a marital relationship where the deliberate setting of short-term, mid-term and long-term plans for marriage is important. A spouse should respect that a partner will not do anything to cause hurt. Consideration and esteeming the partner should be the focus of constantly reflecting to ensure an absence of hurt or pain which may have resulted due to neglect or betrayal of actions or reactions, and words or deeds. A commitment to marriage should cause a spouse to be chaste in sexual behavior in a world that has become increasingly sexually permissive and self-pleasing.

Compassion

Compassion will make a big difference in marriage in the development of a forgiving attitude. There is a need to forgive and receive forgiveness. Possession of compassion results in continuous reflection. Giving will be characteristic of one's relationship where hospitality and charity will be demonstrated.

When a spouse is compassionate a partner's mistakes will be placed in perspective. Being compassionate is to be able to see the bigger picture in the ability to empathize and create an atmosphere of care to rebuild trust and confidence in the relationship. True compassion will cause a spouse to enter the world of his or her partner and be moved to act positively in the best interest of a partner from the product thinking perspective.

ATTITUDE TOWARDS MONEY

In reviewing the marital literature, there is a paucity of discussion of the issue of money. Money as a subject is really important in the life of persons. An analysis of this issue is essential as it is a source of problem in marital relationship. A proper attitude to money is therefore important in building an egalitarian marriage. Product thinking is an important philosophical guide in the development of an appropriate attitude to money in a marriage relationship.

Family therapists and researchers have reported that financial issues rank among the top contributing factors to divorce (Dakin and Wampler, 2008). Persons are often dissatisfied with their entire relationship when they are failing financially. Money is intertwined in marriage and family dynamics. Dakin and Wampler (2008) state that financial stress can include cognitive, emotional, and behavioral responses that affect the relationship and cause a number of marital issues (p. 300).

A poor attitude towards money can cause spousal hostility and affect warmth as it can affect marital satisfaction and stability by poor financial management. Men and women feel and behave differently towards money, which can affect how family finances are handled. Money establishes the egalitarian principle of the relationship, the balance of power. Finally, marital satisfaction increases when wife exercises more influence over the handling of family finances because the wife feels secure when she knows what is happening and also when she participates in decision making re finances.

Couples are more satisfied when they perceive that they are properly handling their finances. The earning potential of a couple will affect areas of satisfaction with a marriage such as investing and building family income which affect marital stability. Although Dakin and Wampler's (2008) study must be accepted with caution due to statistical methodology (couples were all from a clinical sample), it presents support for the literature that asserts that "finances are an important factor in marital satisfaction" (p. 307). The study further notes that low income is correlated with low level of marital satisfaction and higher psychological distress.

These findings show that finances must be properly and carefully managed in the marriage. It may be one of the factors that have a significant positive or negative impact on a relationship. Money is a personal issue for each person within a relationship. Individuals must exercise self-control in order to control spending. This can be achieved because impulsive spending (or overspending problem) can be dealt with successfully (Paulsen et al., 1977).

In an egalitarian marriage built on product thinking, there is always an attitude of joint ownership in expressions. Product thinking is applicable even in a marriage where there is a prenuptial arrangement. However, if the reason for a prearranged prenuptial arrangement is based on a pessimistic attitude then it can be destructive to the marital relationship. Prenuptial arrangement must not extenuate product thinking.

Issues to do with money can cause arguments. Jordan et al. (1999) suggest that "no matter what stage of their relationship, most couples report struggles with money. In fact, money starts more arguments than any other issue" (p 42). Many areas of life, such as childrearing, education, entertainment and vacationing are directly connected to money which makes it highly possible for money to create problems if it is not properly handled. A proper mental attitude towards financial issues is essential to prevent arguments. An if it is "mine" it is yours; if it is "yours" it is mine approach seems to be effective. It does not matter how much I earn, it is "yours." It does not matter how much you earn, it is "mine." This kind of product thinking is crucial for the health of a marital relationship particularly with reference to dual career couples. Product thinking does not work against individual financial freedom when the concept of individual allowance is properly integrated into the dynamics of the pooling of resources.

To control money, one needs to know where one's money is going. It is important for a couple to assess how money is spent in the relationship by each partner for one month. The couple can then use the findings as the benchmark for deciding what needs to be cut and what needs to be treated as priority. It is believed that building family financial security is positively correlated with marital stability. Therefore, as a couple does the assessment the couple should be thinking about saving and investment as vital components of the budget. The secret to wealth creation is to always spend less than one earns and never allow one's self to live from "hand to mouth" or allow all one's pay check to be used for paying bills or debts.

It is important that one has the right attitude towards debt. One should use other persons' money to increase one's own wealth by borrowing money for investment and not for mere pleasure. Therefore, whenever one borrows she or he should ensure that it is for the purpose of increasing assets. A person should also pay off debt as soon as possible and do not practice to lend money without clear terms and conditions. In addition, an individual should not allow others to live off him or her by becoming an "automated money machine." Research has shown that giving to a cause can be very satisfying. Therefore, one should practice to give but be wise about it.

The following principles should be taken into consideration when dealing with family finances. First, decide on how much the couple will give. Second, discuss how much to invest as a partnership. Third, decide on how much to save. Fourth, a consensus should be made regarding the number of special projects. Fifth, decide on how much to spend for living expenses. Sixth, personal allowances should also be discussed as a part of financial planning. Seventh, decide on how to treat additional income. Eighth and final, be frugal in the use of resources; learn to conserve by finding all creative means of saving by spending less. An important caveat is warranted; couples should always fit their budget in their income.

It is important that a couple be very careful as one exercises frugality in order to avoid becoming a miser. A couple should be prudent in the use of resources but not become parsimonious so that the children get the wrong impression. However, never become prodigal or wasteful.

A good approach may be that the couple decides on a percentage of the income for each category discussed and follow the plan. Remember that as a couple, the aims are to invest and save as much as possible at all times. Discuss finances on a monthly basis. Pool resources, don't just split expenses. A couple should establish agreed-on principles for dealing with money because it is an emotionally sensitive issue (Jordan et al., 1999). The system that is agreed on should create balance so that it empowers the couple. Finally, the couple should be so empowered that there is a sense of interdependence that nevertheless creates "independence" based on the product thinking paradigm.

13

Conclusion

THE PREVAILING CONCEPTUALIZATION OF marriage continues to foster patriarchy with concomitant high marital failure. The current conceptualization is based on sum thinking. In sum thinking, the male and female fail to see each other as a part of herself or himself instead of integral and unique individuality. The male or female sees his or her marriage partner as an addition to himself or herself. There is no understanding and internalization of how the male and female come together in marriage to form a so called "joint humanity." Sum thinking therefore perpetuates individualism, which is wreaking havoc on marriage, given the socio-cultural shifts.

The new horizon of product thinking will radically transform one's conceptualization of marriage. This perspective radically changes one's thought about marriage because one begins to recognize that whenever he or she does anything for his or her partner he or she is actually doing it for himself or herself. Product thinking, compassion and awareness are essential ingredients for a successful marriage in this period of human history and for future generations. Product thinking as a revolutionary concept, suggests a revamped philosophical understanding of the phenomenon of marriage as one of the most complex areas of human behavior and social organization. The fact that life is filled with many challenges means that marriage may be viewed as a source of both bane and blessing.

Traditional and liberal societies have been plagued with contributing socio-cultural factors that engender a high rate of divorce and remarriage. Product thinking is the prima facie panacea for even troubled marriages. The marital literature is replete with incidences of past marital success. However, the haunting specter of patriarchy has threatened to upstage that legacy with a counter cultural onslaught on marital unions since the era of savagery to the dawn of civilization. A radical paradigm shift of cognitive proportions is warranted to change prevailing and entrenched social attitudes towards the institution of marriage. The birth of product thinking as an emerging empirical concept will mitigate the détente between redefining cultural influences and that of traditional theological thought. The criteria for marital success are best fulfilled in an egalitarian relationship which is the epitome of product thinking.

Throughout this book, arguments have been made for a new direction for continuous marital success in this postmodern epoch. It has been demonstrated that sum thinking is bankrupt and in its place, product thinking should become the cynosure of marital relationship due to the balance and interest that it generates. Furthermore it should become the denouement of the marital mystery in that product thinking engenders marital happiness and prevents a marriage from becoming an encumbrance. The caveat necessary at this point is the reminder that although the individual couple is focused on explanations to allow for clarity, the recognition of the role that each person plays in the relationship should not be interpreted as separateness but oneness that recognizes the functions of each part.

The review of the historicity of marriage as a patriarchal legacy has exposed the withering stranglehold that patriarchy has had on the soul of humanity's cognitive and cultural mindset. It gave credence to the truism that egalitarianism is the way forward. Product thinking therefore is the sum total of equanimity, which is a necessary tool for establishing an egalitarian marital relationship.

Due to the predisposition for individualism in the Western Hemisphere, product thinking blunts the accepted individualistic mindset to become nugatory. Therefore, the relationship will not be controlled by egocentric behavior, but it will engender a wave of reciprocity through the idealism of product thinking and egalitarianism. Egalitarianism as a cultural concept, allows for effective and efficient implementation of instrumental and expressive leadership roles. This is integral to the function of any small social group, including the marriage relationship.

There is a proven need for the exercise of compassion in the marital relationship. An understanding of human brokenness and bondage should promote the pathos for the expression of compassion in a marital relationship. A lack of compassion and a failure to meet emotional needs often give rise to persons becoming moribund. This is destructive to a marital relationship because a lack of forgiveness portends marital failure but product thinking and compassion are strong socio-cultural, cognitive and emotional cords to create a resilient marriage. A compassionate person can be sensitive to the needs of others, including the need to be healed from hurts and pains.

Compassion as a component of product thinking is the bulwark of a marital relationship because it enables a couple to exercise conciliatory gestures to each other. Thus product thinking along with compassion makes a couple coalesce with the theology of forgiveness as the purging agent in a marital relationship.

With the psychological emotion of compassion as the forerunner, intimacy, passion, and commitment are the other key components of marital love. The practice of compassion within the marital relationship will evoke greater commitment, passion and intimacy. The compassionate attitude of a spouse makes him or her become appeasable and may lead to the development of forbearance. An absence or failure to practice compassion can cause a person to both implode and explode.

Unlike its counterpart, sum thinking is deleterious to a marriage relationship while product thinking is salubrious. Product thinking engenders fealty for the longevity of a marital relationship. Product thinking prevents a spouse from becoming negligent by allowing her or him to consciously pay attention to the portents of marital success discussed. The onus will be therefore on both partners to engage in product thinking as a way of life in order to build a true egalitarian relationship. Such practice of the egalitarian ideal will prevent the relationship from becoming onerous.

Product thinking in itself is not a panacea for marital problems. The paradox is that it can become a panacea if there is motivational engagement in the right kind of product thinking in order to strengthen the true egalitarian ideal. Product thinking motivates a spouse to be determined not to make the mistakes of the past by falling prey to the dictates of a patriarchal value system of gender and social relationships. There is an insatiable desire to learn and apply the principles of marital success. It prompts a spouse to become resolute that he or she will not continue to perpetuate the enslaving patriarchal legacy by deliberately establishing an egalitarian relationship.

In order for a marital relationship to be successful, it must be protected from the invasion of sum thinking, which is entrenched in patriarchy. It must also be safeguarded against the infiltration of lack of compassion and patriarchy. To prevent the invasion and infiltration of marriage, product thinking, compassion and egalitarianism must become the way of thinking, feeling and acting in a marriage relationship in this and successive generations because one's conceptualization of marriage has significant impact on his or her attitudes in the marital relationship.

Sum thinking is cultivated and nurtured by the patriarchal approach. This is so because the patriarchal approach allows a spouse to think in separated terms. It keeps marriage partners separated at the cognitive and behavioral levels. This causes the male to treat the female as inferior and perpetuates the crippling effects of the patriarchal legacy.

In product thinking, one's metaphors of marriage help her or him to resolutely take responsibility for her or his attitudes and actions. Product thinking is diametrically opposed to sum thinking and patriarchy. Product thinking is therefore the foundation of the egalitarian ideal that the socio-cultural changes demand.

The marriage literature is replete with evidence that sum thinking is destructive to a marriage relationship. Sum thinking perpetuates individualism and the enslaving patriarchal legacy. If product thinking replaces sum thinking marriage can be radically transformed because product thinking allows one to intentionally care for the total well-being of one's partner until it becomes second nature. Therefore, product thinking will prevent the perpetuation of common problems associated with marital failures. It will also counteract marital failures by positively impacting the common reasons given for marital failures.

The review of the love phenomenon revealed that the prevailing conceptualizations of love are inadequate due to failure to deal with the construct of compassion as well as being able to pass the philosophical test of existence. It was therefore established that the ideal marital love must have compassion as its basis along with the three other key elements of passion, commitment and intimacy in high proportion. Product thinking deepens marital love because it affects one's attitudes at both the conscious and unconscious levels. Product thinking results in a redefinition of marital love that fosters the egalitarian ideal and profoundly impacts how one understands and expresses his or her sexuality in marriage and in relation to the opposite sex.

The analysis of the concept of the collective unconscious revealed that patriarchy is deeply ingrained in the history of humanity. Therefore, even well-intentioned individuals continue to perpetuate patriarchy based on shared experiences throughout the centuries which continue to operate at the unconscious level. Product thinking is potent enough to upstage the patriarchal collective unconscious and create an egalitarian mindset that can usher in a new collective unconscious in successive generations. Product thinking needs to be vigorously pursued until it becomes woven in the fabric of humanity's collective unconscious.

Product thinking generates a recasting of the Golden Rule in relation to marriage. Ushered in by product thinking, the Golden Rule of Marriage becomes "do unto yourself as you would have yourself do unto you." Product thinking causes one to acknowledge that one's partner is a part of one's own self. Therefore, whenever one does something for one's partner one is actually doing it for herself or himself. This Golden Rule of marriage, guided by product thinking, compassion and egalitarianism, will transform a marital relationship from egocentric reciprocity to reciprocity within the union, which is actually reciprocity within the self.

Finally, product thinking has the potential to become a potent philosophical underpinning of one's life and marriage because it fosters successive approximations. This is so because it allows one to celebrate incremental accomplishments and take progressive steps towards goal attainment. This is best illustrated by the attitude necessary to run a marathon. If the runner focuses on the many miles to be run he or she might become discouraged, but if he or she keeps telling himself or herself "just one more mile" he or she will be continuously motivated throughout the marathon. One should therefore keep perspective on his or her marriage and celebrate successive approximations until she or he attains the egalitarian ideal to which everyone should aspire.

Glossary

Automaticity: A mental process in which one cares for his/her partner without conscious effort.

Blended family: A basic societal unit in which there are children from a previous marriage.

Cognitive restructuring: the process of replacing dysfunctional and destructive thought patterns with healthy thoughts through knowledge and introspection.

Collective unconscious: all the things about the human race that continue to affect us at the unconscious level.

Communal marriage: The marriage between single men and women without any exclusive cohabitation right.

Communication: The process of attending to information through various media and methods in order to serve one's interests as well as the interests of others.

Compassion: A decision to bear with persons out of recognition that there is always the threat of human failure but choosing to maintain willingness to offer as well as receive forgiveness.

Complementation: The recognition that both male and female have personal resources that complement each other and enable them to contribute meaningfully to each other's well-being.

Conflict: A state that results when one believes that his/her interest(s) is not being served or will not be served, based on internal and or external factor(s).

Costs and benefits: The belief that one's own satisfaction and gratification are important factors in the attraction spectrum.

Cycle of love making: A systematic approach that helps couples to improve the process of love making in order to increase sexual intimacy.

Dual-career relationship: A relationship in which both partners are employed outside of the home in order to contribute economically.

Egalitarian relationship: A cohabitation in which partners believe that male and female are equal and as a result share equally in family duties, responsibilities, and decision making.

Egalitarianism: The philosophy that male and female are equal and should be given equal opportunities as well as treated equally in all spheres of life and human endeavors.

Empowerment: The commitment to promote the self-actualization of a person by encouraging and supporting the discovery and development of skills and abilities.

Endogamy: A marriage to a person within the group to which one belongs.

Equanimity: An attitude of full acceptance of equality between the sexes.

Exogamy: A marriage to a person outside of the group to which one belongs.

Family: A culturally and theologically guided phenomenon, which refers to a basic unit in society where its members are related by blood, marriage and possibly adoption, in which the primary functions include sexual relation and or reproduction and or child-rearing, economic partnership, the shaping of character through religious and or other forms of education and training, and the empowerment of its members.

Forgiveness: A personal responsibility to let go of hurt and resentment and respond to the offender in a loving way, which involves a move from negative emotions to positive emotions.

Group marriage: "All the women in one class are regarded as the actual, or at all events potential, wives of all the men in another class" (Ellis, 1910, p. 423).

Imagineering: A seasonal state in which one looks at the past in celebration or disappointment and plans for the future with anxiety or hope.

Intentionality: The deliberate actions performed in order to achieve a specific outcome.

Intimacy: The close bond that exists between persons, which increases in intensity as they increase self-disclosure and become more vulnerable with each other.

Johari window of love: A concept that utilizes the Johari window to explain the different kinds of love, in which there is aimless love, associative love, accommodative love, and authentic love based on the level of the four components of love.

Judeo-Christian: The religious beliefs and system of the Jews upon which Christianity is founded.

Looking glass self: A concept that states that we come to see ourselves how others see us.

Love: A phenomenon made up of the elements of passion, commitment, intimacy, and compassion in which the level of intensity of those elements plays an integral role in determining the quality of love.

Marital communication: A deliberate process of tuning in to one's partner, which involves attending, engaging, connecting, processing, prospecting, and concluding.

Marriage: The universally accepted cohabitation of a male and female who are joined together as wife and husband, based on cultural and or religious principles.

Matching phenomenon: "The tendency for men and women to choose as partners those who are a 'good match' in attractiveness and other traits" (Myers, 2005, p. 433).

Matriarchy: The philosophy that females are not inferior to males and should be allowed personal freedom in all spheres of life and human endeavors.

Matrifocal family: A basic societal unit in which a woman is the chief leader.

Metaphors of marriage: Comparisons geared at helping to understand important marital principles as they are extremely useful in painting pictures of reality.

Monogamy: The marriage of single pairs.

Paradigm shift: A new way of seeing, understanding, internalizing, and acting in male-female relationships.

Patriarchy: The philosophy that male is superior to female and male should rule over female in all spheres of life and human endeavors.

Patrifocal: A basic societal unit in which a man is the chief leader.

Physical attractiveness: An evaluative judgment of beauty, which is dependent on cultural understanding, as well as one's own standards of judgment. Whatever one's culture presents as attractive impacts one's own understanding of attractiveness.

Polyandry: A marriage in which one woman has several husbands simultaneously.

Polygamy: The marriage of one man to more than one woman or the marriage of one woman to more than one man.

Polygyny: The marriage of one man to two or more women simultaneously.

Presuppositions: The assumptions including beliefs and values that govern one's life at the conscious or unconscious level.

Product thinking: The application of the mathematical principle of product to explain the mental process in which one sees his/her partner as a crucial part of his/her whole, not just a mere addition, which results in interdependence.

Proximity: The accessibility that provides a vital link to geographical distance and how often persons come in contract.

Reciprocity of liking effect: The belief that we have the proclivity to like those who like us.

Re-socialization: The process of replacing gender bias, especially the treatment of females as inferior to males, with gender equality where there is no longer a glorification of the masculine and devaluation of the feminine.

Sexuality: The essence of being human, which encompasses one's values, emotions, desires, and drive towards love and deep affection.

Spiritual equality: The belief that God sees men and women as equal in Jesus Christ.

Sum thinking: The application of the mathematical principle of sum to explain the mental process in which one sees his/her partner as a mere addition to him/herself, which results in continued independence.

The golden rule of marriage: Do unto yourself as you would have yourself do unto you.

The looking-glass self: A concept that states that we come to see ourselves how others see us.

Trial marriage: An unmarried cohabitation in which the couple's commitment is based on relationship satisfaction, size of investment, and the quality of alternatives.

Wheel theory of love: A theory that states that love has four components: rapport, self-revelation, mutual dependency, and personality and need fulfillment. In a serious, long-lasting intimate relationship, the wheel will turn indefinitely; it may turn only a few times in a short-lived romance and the weight of each component cause the wheel to move forward or backward.

Bibliography

Adams, J. M., & Jones, W. H. (1997). The *conceptualization of marital commitment: An integrative analysis*. Journal of Personality and Social Psychology, 72(5), 1177–1196. Retrieved September 2, 2008, from the PsycNET database.

Adler, R. B., & Elmhorst, R. B. (2005). *Communicating at work: principles and practices for business and the profession (8th ed.)*. Boston: McGraw-Hill.

Archer, G. L. (1994). *A Survey of Old Testament introduction (Rev.)*. Chicago: Moody Press.

Arlandson, J. M. (1997). *Women, class, and society in early Christianity: Models from Luke–Acts*. Peabody, MI: Hendrickson Publishers, Inc.

Arthur, K. (2000). *A Marriage without regrets*. Eugene, Oregon: Harvest House Publishers.

Balswick, J. O., & Balswick J. K. (1999). *The family: A Christian perspective on the contemporary home (2nd ed.)*. Grand Rapids, Michigan: Baker Books.

Baran, S. J. (2004). *Introduction to mass communication: Media literacy and culture (3rd ed.)*. Boston: McGraw-Hill.

Baron, R. A., & Byrne, D. (2000). *Social psychology (9th ed.)*. Boston: Allyn and Bacon.

Basson, R. (2000). "The female sexual response: a different model," [Electronic version]. Journal of Sex & Marital Therapy, 26, 51–65. Retrieved October 4, 2006, from Academic Search Premier database.

Basson, R. (2001a). "Human sex-response cycle," [Electronic version]. Journal of Sex & Marital Therapy, 27, 33–43. Retrieved October 4, 2006, from Academic Search Premier database.

Basson, R. (2001b). "Using a different model for female sexual response to address women's problematic low sexual desire," [Electronic version]. Journal of Sex & Marital Therapy, 27, 395–403. Retrieved October 4, 2006, from Academic Search Premier database.

Baucom, D. H. (2001). "Religion and the science of relationships: Is a happy marriage possible?" Journal of Family Psychology, 15(4), 652–656). Retrieved September 9, 2008, from the PsycNET database.

Bauer, W. (1979). *A Greek-English lexicon of the New Testament and other early Christian literature* (W. F. Arndt & F. W. Gingrich, trans.). Chicago: The University of Chicago Press. (Original work published 1958)

Beck, J. G., Bozman, A. W., & Qualtrough, T. *(1991)*. "The Experience of Sexual Desire: Psychological Correlates in a College Sample" [Electronic version]. Journal of Sex Research 28(3), 443–356. Retrieved October 7, 2008, from Academic Search Premier Database.

Benjamin, L. T. Jr., Whitaker, J. L., Ramsey, R. M., & Zeve, D. R. (2007). "John B. Watson alleged sex research" [Abstract]. American Psychologists, 62(2), 131–131. Retrieved October 6, 2008, from Academic Search Premier database.

Benner, D. G. (2003). *Surrender to love: Discovering the heart of Christian spirituality.* Downers Grove, IL: Intervarsity Press.

Benner, D. G. (2005). *Desiring God's will: Aligning our hearts with the heart of God.* Downers Grove, IL: Intervarsity Press.

Bentler, P. M., & Newcomb, M. D. (1978). "Longitudinal study of marital success and failure." Journal of Consulting and Clinical Psychology, 46 (5), 1053–1070). Retrieved September 9, 2008, from the PsycNET database.

Benton, J. (2000). *Gender questions: Biblical manhood and womanhood in the contemporary world.* Auburn, MA: Evangelical Press.

Bilezikian, G. (1985). *Beyond sex roles: What the bible says about women's place in the church and family (2nd ed.).* Grand Rapids, Michigan: Baker Book House.

Boomsma, C. (1993). *Male and female, one in Christ: New Testament teaching on women in office.* Grand Rapids, Michigan: Baker Book House.

Bruni, E. (1974). Psychotherapists as sex therapists. Psychotherapy: Theory, Research & Practice, 11(3), 277–281. Retrieved October 6, 2008, from PsycNET database.

Carson, B. (1992). *Think big: Unleashing your potential for excellence.* Grand Rapids, Michigan: Zondervan.

Carter, H. L. J., & Foley, L. (1943). "What are young people asking about marriage?" Journal of Applied Psychology, 27(3), 275–282. Retrieved September 9, 2008, from the PsycNET database.

Carter, B., & Peters J. K. (1998). "Remaking marriage and family." Marriage and Family Annual Editions, 36, 176–181.

Chambers, M., Hanawalt, B., Herlihy, D. Rabb, T. K., Woloch, I., & Grew R. (1999). *The western experience (7th ed.).* Boston, Illinois: McGraw-Hill College.

Chapman, G. (2004). *The five love languages: How to express heartfelt commitment to your mate.* Chicago: Northfield Publishing.

Chasteen, K., & Kissman, K. (2000). "Juggling multiple roles and the act of resistance." Contemporary Family Therapy, 22(2), 233–240. Retrieved October 8, 2008, from Academic Search Premier database.

Clinebell, H. (1984). *Basic types of pastoral care and counseling: Resources for the ministry of healing and growth (Rev.).* Nashville: Abingdon Press.

Collins, G. R. (1988). *Christian counseling: A comprehensive guide (Rev. ed.).* USA: W Publishing Group.

Com-. (2008). *In Merriam-Webster Online Dictionary.* Retrieved October 24, 2008, from http://www.merriam-webster.com/dictionary/com-

Compassion. (2008). *In Merriam-Webster Online Dictionary.* Retrieved October 24, 2008, from http://www.merriam-webster.com/dictionary/compassion

Cook, W. L., & Douglas, E. M. (1998). "The looking-glass self in family context: A social relations analysis." Journal of Family Psychology, 12(3), 299–309. Retrieved October 12, 2008, from PsycNET database.

Corey, G. (2000). *Theory and practice of group counseling (5th ed.).* USA: Brooks/cole, Thomson Learning.

Covey, S. R. (1989, 2004). *The 7 habits of highly effective people: Restoring the character ethic.* New York: Free Press.

Covey, S. R. (2004). *The 8th habit: From effectiveness to greatness.* New York: Free Press.

Crary, D. (2007). "U.S. divorce rate falls to lowest level since 1970, but why?" Associated Press. Retrieved September 27, 2008, from http://www.boston.com/news/local/new

_hampshire/articles/2007/05/10/us_divorce_rate_fallsto_lowest_level_since_1970_but_why/

Curran, D. (1983). *Traits of a healthy family*. Minneapolis, Minnesota: USA.

Dakin, J., & Wampler, R. (2008). "Money doesn't buy happiness, but it helps: Marital satisfaction, psychological distress, and demographic differences between low- and middle-income clinic couples" [Electronic version]. The American Journal of Family Therapy, 36, 300–311. Retrieved December 22, 2008, from Academic Search Premier database.

Davey, A., Fincham, F. D., Beach, S. R. H., & Brody, G. H. (2001). "Attribution in marriage: Examining the entailment model in dyadic context." Journal of Family Psychology, 15(4), 721–734. Retrieved September 9, 2008, from the PsycNET database.

Davidson, B. S. (1992). *Before they say I do: A handbook for counsellors (2nd ed.)*. Kingston, Jamaica: Family Life Ministries.

DeLamater, J., Hyde, J. S., & Fong, M.-C. (2008). "Sexual satisfaction in the seventh decade of life" [Abstract]. Journal of Sex & Marital Therapy, 34(5). Retrieved October 7, 2008, from Academic Search Premier database.

Devine, D., & Forehand, R. (1996). "Cascading towards divorce: The roles of marital and child factors." Journal of Counseling and Clinical Psychology, 64(2), 424–427). Retrieved September 9, 2008, from the PsycNET database.

Dobson, K. S. (Ed.). (2001). *Handbook of cognitive behavioral Therapies (2nd ed.)*. New York: The Guilford Press.

Dunlap, K. (1935). "Marriage and the family". In *K. Dunlap, Civilized life: The principles and applications of social psychology* (pp. 134–181). Baltimore, MD, US: Williams & Wilkins Co. Retrieved September 9, 2008, from the PsycNET database.

Economist (1994). "Not much of it about" [Abstract]. Economist, 333(7885), 28–28. Retrieved October 7, 2008, from Academic Search Premier database.

Ellis, H. (1910). "Marriage." In *H. Ellis, Sex in relations to societies* (pp. 420–506). Philadelphia, PA, US: F A Davis. Retrieved September 9, 2008, from the PsycNET database.

Engels, F. (1972). *The origin of the family, private property and the state: Edited, with an introduction by Eleanor Burke Leacock*. New York: International Publishers.

Enright, R. D., & Fitzgibbons, R. P. (2000). "Forgiveness in Marital and Family Therapy." In *R. D. Enright, & R. P. Fitzgibbons, Helping clients forgive: An empirical guide for resolving anger and restoring hope* (pp. 193–214). Washington, DC, US: American Psychological Association. Retrieved September 9, 2008, from PsycNET database.

Enright, R. D., & Fitzgibbons, R. P. (2000). "The moral, philosophical, and religious roots of forgiveness." In *R. D. Enright, & R. P. Fitzgibbons, Helping clients forgive: An empirical guide for resolving anger and restoring hope* (pp. 253–266). Washington, DC, US: American Psychological Association. Retrieved September 9, 2008, from PsycNET database.

Farrar, S. (1990). *Point man: How a man can lead his family*. USA: Multnomah Books.

Feldman, R. S. (2005). *Essentials of understanding psychology (6th ed.)*. NY: McGraw-Hill.

Fincham, F. D., Beach, S. R. H., & Davila, J. (2004). "Forgiveness and conflict resolution in marriage." Journal of Family Psychology, 18(1), 72–81. Retrieved September 9, 2008, from PsycNET database.

Fincham, F. D., Beach, S. R. H., & Davila, J. (2007). "Longitudinal relationship between forgiveness and conflict resolution." Journal of Family Psychology, 21(1), 542–545. Retrieved September 9, 2008, from PsycNET database.

Firestone, R. W., Firestone, L. A., & Catlett, J. (2006). "Factors that affect an individual's sexuality." In *R. W. Firestone, L. A. Firestone, J. Catlett, Sex and love in intimate relationships* (pp. 43-74). Washington, DC: American Psychological Association. Retrieved September 9, 2008, from the PsycNET database.

Frank, E., & Brandstätter, V. (2002). "Approach versus avoidance: different types of commitment in intimate relationships." Journal of Personality and Social Psychology, 82(2), 208-221). Retrieved September 9, 2008, from the PsycNET database.

Ganong, W. F. (1973). *Review of Medical Physiology (6th 4d.)*. Los Altos, California: Large Medical Publications.

Gaskiyane, I. (2000). *Polygamy: A cultural and Biblical perspective*. United Kingdom: Piquant.

Gattis, K. S., Berns, S., Simpson, L. E., & Christensen, A. (2004). "Birds of a feather or strange birds? Ties among personality dimensions, similarity, and marital quality." Journal of Family Psychology, 18(4), 564-574). Retrieved September 2, 2008, from the PsycNET database.

Gillette, J. M., & Reinhardt, J. M. (1942). "The family and marriage in the new age." In *J. M. Gillette, & J. M. Reinhardt, Problems of a changing social order* (pp. 549-581). New York, US: American Book Company. Retrieved September 9, 2008, from the PsycNET database.

Goldman, B. (1994). "The essence of attraction." Health, Retrieved October 2, 2008, from Academic Search Premier database.

Gonzaga, G. C., Turner, R. A., Keltner, D., Campos, B., & Altermus, M. (2006). "Romantic Love and Sexual Desire in Close Relationships." Emotion, 6(2), 163-179. Retrieved September 9, 2008, from PsycNET database.

Greeff, A. P., & Malherbe, H. L. (2001). "Intimacy and marital satisfaction in spouses." Journal of Sex & Marital Therapy, 27, 247-257. Retrieved October 7, 2008, from Academic Search Premier database.

Gray, J. (1992). *Men are from mars, women are from venus: The classic guide to understanding the opposite sex*. New York: Harper Collins Publishers Inc.

Green, D. S. (2006). *Breaking free: The key to empowerment, happiness and fulfillment - A Caribbean perspective*. Kingston, Jamaica: LMH Publishing Limited.

Gupta, S., & Lynch, J. (2002). "The chemistry of love." Time, 159(7), 78. Retrieved October 2, 2008, from Academic Search Premier database.

Hansen, J. C., Rossberg, R. H., & Cramer, S. H. (1994). *Counseling theory and process (5th ed.)*. Boston: Allyn and Bacon.

Haralambos, M., & Holborn, M. (1995). *Sociology: Themes and perspectives (4th ed.)*. Hammersmith, London: Collins Educational.

Harley, W. F. (1997). *His needs, her needs: Building an affair-proof marriage*. Great Britain: Monarch Publications.

Hasker, W. (1983). *Metaphysics: Constructing a world view*. Downers Grove, Illinois: Intervarsity Press.

Hassebrauck, M., & Buhl, T. (1996). "Three-dimensional love." Journal of Social Psychology, 136(1), 121-122. Retrieved October 3, 2008, from Academic Search Premier database.

Hove, R. (1999). *Equality in Christ? Galatians 3:28 and the gender dispute*. Wheaton, Illinois: Crossway Books.

Hurley, J. B. (1981). *Man and woman in biblical perspective*. Grand Rapids, MI: Zondervan Publishing House.

Jewett, P. K. (1975). *Man as male and female*. Grand Rapids: William B. Eerdmans Publishing Company.

Johnson, A. G. (1997). *The gender knot: Unraveling our patriarchal legacy*. Philadelphia: Temple University Press.

Jones, S. L., & Butman, R. (1991). *Modern Psychotherapies: A comprehensive Christian appraisal*. Downers Grove, Illinois: Intervarsity Press.

Jordan, P. L., Stanley, S. M., & Markman, H. J. (1999). *Becoming parents: How to strengthen your marriage as your family grows*. San Francisco: Jossey-Bass.

Kakin, J., & Wampler, R. (2008). "Money doesn't buy happiness, but it helps: Marital satisfaction, psychological distress, and demographic differences between low – and middle-income clinic couples" [Electronic version]. The American Journal of Family Therapy, 36, 300–311.

Kita, J. (1998). "Keep it up." Men's Health, 13(10), 130. Retrieved October 7, 2008, from Academic Search Premier database.

Keener, C. S. (1992). *Paul, women & wives: Marriage and women's ministry in the letters of Paul*. Peabody, Massachusetts: Hendrickson Publishers, Inc.

Kelley, E. L., & Conley, J. J. (1987). "Personality and compatibility: A prospective analysis of marital stability and marital satisfaction." Journal of Personality and Social Psychology, 52(1), 27–40). Retrieved September 2, 2008, from the PsycNET database.

Kroeger, C. C. & Beck, J. R. (Eds.). (1996). *Women, abuse and the bible: How scripture can be used to hurt and heal*. Grand Rapids, MI: Baker Books.

Levinger, G., & Breedlove, J. (1960). "Interpersonal attraction and agreement: A study of marriage partners." Journal of Personality and Social Psychology, 3(4), 367–372. Retrieved September 9, 2008, from PsycNET database.

Lewis Henry Morgan. (2008). *In Encyclopedia Britannica*. Retrieved October 12, 2008, from Encyclopedia Britannica Online: http://www.britannica.com/EBchecked/topic/392246/Lewis-Henry-Morgan

Lewin, K. (1997). "The background of conflict in marriage (1940)." In *K. Lewin, Resolving social conflicts and field theory in social science* (pp. 68–79). Washington, DC: American Psychological Association. Retrieved September 9, 2008, from the PsycNET database.

MacKinnon, C. (1989*). Feminism Unmodified: Discourses on Life and Law*. Cambridge: Harvard University Press.

MacKinnon, C. (1987). *Toward a Feminist Theory of the State*. Cambridge: Harvard University Press MacKinnon.

Magoun, H. W. (1981). "John B. Watson and the study of human sexual behavior," [Electronic version]. The Journal of Sex Research, 17(4), 368–378. Retrieved October 4, 2008, form Academic Search Premier database.

Maio, G. R., Thomas, G., Fincham, F. D., & Carnelley, K. B. (2008). "Unraveling the role of forgiveness in family relationships." Journal of personality and social psychology, 94(2), 307–319. Retrieved September 9, 2008, from PsycNET database.

Markhman, H., Halford, K., & Lindahl, K. (2000). "Marriage." In *A. E. Kazdin (Ed.), Encyclopedia of psychology* (Vol. 5, pp. 109–114). Washington, DC, US: American Psychological Association; Oxford University Press. Retrieved September 9, 2008, from the PsycNET database.

Marriage Partnership. (1995). "The older the better?" [Abstract] Marriage Partnership, 12 (3), 68–68. Retrieved October 7, 2008, from Religion and Philosophy Collection database.

Masters, W. H., & Johnson, V. E. (1966). Human Sexual response> Boston: Little Browne & Co.

McCarthy, B. W. (1973). "A modification of Masters and Johnson sex therapy model in a clinical setting." Psychotherapy: Theory, Research & Practice, 10(4), 290–293. Retrieved October 6, 2008, from PsycNET database.

McDowell, J. (1996). *The father connection: 10 qualities of the heart that empower your children to make right choices*. Nashville, Tennessee: Broadman & Holman Publishers.

McGee, R., (1980). *Sociology: An introduction (2nd ed.)*. New York: Holt, Rinehart and Winston.

McNulty, J. K. (2008). "Forgiveness in marriage: Putting the benefits into context." Journal of Family Psychology, 22(1), 171–175. Retrieved September 9, 2008, from PsycNET database.

Morgan, L. H. (1877). *Ancient Society*. London.

Mudd, E. H. (with Goodwin, H. M., 1963). "Marital problems and adjustment." In A. Deutch, & H. Fishman (Eds.), *The Encyclopedia of Mental Health* (Vol. 3, pp. 965-978). New York, US: Franklin Watts. Retrieved September 9, 2008, from the PsycNET database.

Muller, R. A. (1985). *Dictionary of Latin and Greek theological terms: Drawn primarily from protestant scholastic theology*. Grand Rapids, Michigan: Baker Book House.

Mullet, E., Girard, M., & Bakhshi, P. (2004). "Conceptualizing forgiveness." European Psychologist, 9(2), 78–86. Retrieved September 9, 2008, from PsycNET database.

Munce, R. H. (1985). What happened? A study in Genesis. Largo, FL: R. L. Munce Publishing, Inc.

Murray, S. L., & Holmes, J. G. (2000). "Seeing the self through a partner's eyes: Why self-doubts turn into relationship insecurities." In *Abraham Tesser, Richard B. Felson, & Jerry M. Suls (Eds.), Psychological perspectives on self and identity*. (pp. 173–197). Washington, DC, US: American Psychological Association.

Murray, S. L., Holmes, J. G., MacDonald, G., & Ellsworth, P. C. (1998). "Through the looking glass darkly? When self-doubts turns into relationship insecurities." Journal of Personality and Social Psychology, 75(6), 1459–1480. Retrieved October 12, 2008, from PsycNET database.

Myers, D. (2005). *Social Psychology (8th ed.)*. Boston, Illinois: McGraw Hill.

Narramore, C. M. (1960). *The psychology of counseling: Professional techniques for pastors, teachers, youth leaders, and all who are engaged in the incomparable art of counseling*. Grand Rapids, Michigan: Zondervan Publishing House.

Necromancy. (2008). In *Merriam-Webster Online Dictionary*. Retrieved December 20, 2008, from http://www.merriam-webster.com/dictionary/necromancy

Neiger, S. (1966). "Recent trends in sex research: New facts for the clinician: Horizons for the psychologist in research." Canadian Psychologist, 7a(2), 102-114. Retrieved October 6, 2008, from PsycNET database.

Nichols, M. P. (with Schwartz, R. C., 2004). *Family therapy: Concepts and methods (6th ed.)*. Boston: Pearson Education, Inc.

Nisbet, J. F. (1889). "Christianity and morality." In *J. F. Nisbet, Marriage and heredity: A view of psychological evolution* (pp. 35–57). London, England: Ward and Downey. Retrieved September 9, 2008, from the PsycNET database.

Nisbet, J. F. (1989). "Polygamy." In *J. F. Nisbet, Marriage and heredity: A view of psychological evolution* (pp. 186–202). London, England: Ward and Downey. Retrieved September 9, 2008, from the PsycNET database.

Parsons, S. F. (1996). *Feminism and Christian ethics*. Great Britain: Cambridge University Press.

Pasley, K., & Grecas, V. (1984). "Stresses and satisfaction of the parental role." The Personnel and Guidance Journal, 400–404. Retrieved October 8, 2008, from Academic Search Premier database.

Paulsen, K., Rimm, D. C., Woodburn, L. T., & Rimm, S. (1977). "A self-control approach to inefficient spending." Journal of Consulting and Clinical Psychology, 45(3), 433–435. Retrieved October 16, 2008, from PsycNET database.

Pelt, N. V. (1997). *Heart to heart: The art of communication*. Miami, Florida: Inter-American Division Publishing Association.

Perlman, S. D., & Abramson, P. R. (1982). "Sexual satisfaction among married and cohabiting individuals." Journal of Consulting and Clinical Psychology, 1982, 50(3), 458–460. Retrieved October 7, 2008, from PsycNET database.

Pritchard, R. (2005). *The healing power of forgiveness*. Eugene, Oregon: Harvest House Publishers.

Rauch, J. (1998). "For better or worse?" Marriage and Family Annual Editions, 19, 89–94.

Rogers, C. L. Jr., & Rogers, C. L. III. (1998). *The new linguistic and exegetical key to the Greek New Testament*. Grand Rapids, Michigan: Zondervan Publishing House.

Santrock, J. W. (2006). *Life-span development (10th ed.)*. NY: McGraw-Hill.

Schnittger, M. H., & Bird, G. W. (1990). "Coping among dual-career men and women across the family life cycle" [Abstract]. Family Relations, 39(2), 199–205. Retrieved October 8, 2008, from Academic Search Premier database.

Schwartz, P. (1998). "Peer Marriage: What does it take to create a truly egalitarian relationship?" Marriage and Family Annual Editions, 18, 84–88.

Scott, R. L., & Castellani, A. M. (2002). "Prediction 2 – year marital satisfaction from partners' discussion of their marriage check up." Journal of Marriage and Family Therapy, 28(4), 399–407.

Shepard, J. M., & Greene, R. W. (2001). *Sociology and you*. Lincolnwood, Illinois: National Textbook Company.

Storaasli, R. D., & Markman, H. J. (1990). "Relationship problems in the early stages of Marriage: A longitudinal investigation." Journal of Family Psychology, 4(1), 80–98. Retrieved September 9, 2008, from the PsycNET database.

Sue, D., Sue, D., & Sue, S. (1997). *Understanding abnormal behaviour (5th ed.)*. Boston: Houghton Mifflin Company.

Swift, B. (1998). "The work of oneness: How to make marriage a sacred union." Marriage and Family Annual Editions, 21, 101–104.

Talmey, B. S. (1938). "Evolution of marriage from promiscuity to monogamy." In B. S. Talmey, *Love: A treatise on the science of sex-attraction (Rev.)* (pp. 427–434). New York, US: Eugenics Publishing Company. Retrieved September 9, 2008, from the PsycNET database.

Talmey, B. S. (1933, 1938). "Love: A treatise on the science of sex-attraction" (newly revised and enlarged). (pp. 441–458). New York, US: Eugenics Publishing Company. Retrieved September 9, 2008, from PsycNET database.

Tan, S.-Y. (2006). *Full service: Moving from self-serve Christianity to total servanthood*. Grand Rapids, Michigan: Baker Books.

Theories of Family Development. (2004). In *The Concise Corsini Encyclopedia of Psychology and Behavioral Science*. Retrieved October 31, 2009, from http://www.credoreference.com/entry/wileypsych/theories_of_family_development

Tolstedt, B. E., & Stokes, J. P. (1983). "Relationship of verbal, affective, and physical intimacy to marital satisfaction." Journal of Counseling Psychology, 30(2), 573–580). Retrieved September 9, 2008, from the PsycNET database.

Turner, J. F., & Helms, D. B. (1995. *Lifespan development (5th ed.).* Fort Worth: Harcourt Brace College Publishers.

Vine. W. E. (1966). *An expository dictionary of New Testament words.* Old Tappan, New Jersey: Fleming H. Revell Company.

Wallerstein, J. S. (1994). "The early psychological tasks of marriage: Part I." American Journal of Orthopsychiatry, 64(4), 640-650). Retrieved September 9, 2008, from the PsycNET database.

Wallerstein, J. S. (1996). "The psychological tasks of marriage: Part II." American Journal of Orthopsychiatry, 66(2), 217-227. Retrieved September 9, 2008, from the PsycNET database.

Waterfield, R. (1993). *Plato Republic.* Oxford: Oxford University Press. (Original work published c. 427-347BC).

Watson, M., & Davidson, B. S. (2006*). Healthy family: A Caribbean perspective.* Kingston, Jamaica: Family Life Ministries.

Weisfeld, C. C. (1997). "Marriage in cross-cultural perspective." In *N. L. Segal, G. E. Weisfeld, & C. C. Weisfeld (Eds.), Uniting psychology and biology: Integrative perspectives on human development* (pp. 355-367). Washington, DC: American Psychological Association. Retrieved September 9, 2008, from the PsycNET database.

Westermarck, E. A. (1901). *The History of Human Marriage (3rd ed.).* London: Macmillan and Co. Ltd.

Wheat, E. (1983). *How to Save Your Marriage Alone.* Grand Rapids, Michigan: Zondervan Publishing House.

Wheat, E., & Perkins, G. O. (1980). *Love life for every married couple.* Grand Rapids, Michigan: Zondervan Publishing House.

Wheat, E. & Wheat G. (1997). *Intended for Pleasure (3rd ed.).* Grand Rapids, Michigan: Fleming H. Revell.

Whisman, M. A., Dixon, A. E. & Johnson, B. (1997). "Therapists' perspectives of couple problems and treatment issues in couple therapy." Journal of Family Psychology, 11(3), 361–366. Retrieved September 2, 2008 from the PsycNET database.

William A. Fisher, W. A. & Byrne, B. (1978). "Sex Differences in Response to Erotica? Love Versus Lust." Journal of Personality and Social Psychology, 36(2), 117–125). Retrieved September 9, 2008, from PsycNET database.

Wolfe, A. (2008). "Human nature." Retrieved December 8, 2008, from http://www.bookrags.com/research/human-nature-eos-02/>

Worthington, E. L., Jr. (1990). *Counseling before marriage: A how—to approach.* Dallas: Word Publishing.

Yeung, K. T., Martin, J. L. (2003). "The looking glass self: An empirical test and elaboration." Social Forces, 81(3), 843–879. Retrieved October 7, 2008, from Academic Search Premier database.

Young, E. (2003). *The ten commandments of marriage: The do's and don'ts of a lifelong covenant.* Chicago: Moody Publishers.

Subject/Name Index

A

ability, 34, 51, 53, 56, 75, 91, 106, 111, 120, 123, 134
accommodation, 82
adjustment problems, 98
adolescence, 103
affective intimacy, 34, 130
affirmation, 13, 35, 77, 95, 106, 110, 112, 115, 126
Africa, 36, 130
agreement, 5, 26, 37, 60, 153
all-embracing, 77, 82
all-encompassing, 77, 82
answers, 1, 111
anthropological, 15
anthropology, xv, 11
antidote, 99
apology, 113
appreciation, 29, 91, 95, 109, 112, 115
approach, xi, xvi, 2, 3, 4, 18, 22, 26, 41, 67, 73, 88, 107, 125, 135, 136, 140, 144
    egalitarian, 2, 4, 88
    patriarchal, 2, 3, 88, 140
argument(s), xiv, xv, xviii, 4, 16, 21, 22, 135, 138
aspiration, 89, 96
assimilation, 82
atmosphere, 35, 45, 132, 134
attending, 89, 121, 122, 143, 145
attitude, 14, 31, 32, 52, 53, 54, 67, 68, 75, 88, 106, 107, 108, 109, 111, 112, 113, 114, 124, 127, 128, 130, 132, 134, 135, 136, 141, 144
    compassionate, 83, 139
    egalitarian, 35
    forgiving, 133
    individualistic, xvii
    negative, 109, 128
    pessimistic, 135
    positive, 109, 128
    unforgiving, 77
    servanthood, 91
    towards money, 134
attraction, 28, 33, 34, 37, 38, 39, 40, 41, 80, 81, 143
authoritative parents, 103
automaticity, 73, 75, 76, 79, 84, 90, 100, 107, 109, 143

B

banyan tree. See marriage, metaphors of
barbarism, 6, 11, 12, 14, 15, 16
Basson, R., 56, 58, 59, 149
benefits, 39, 89, 91, 143, 154
best friend, 82, 98
blended family. See family, types of
blessing, 84, 91, 137
brake system, 45
Britain, 24
Buddhism, 20, 25, 27

C

capitalism, xiii, xiv, xvi
care, 7, 9, 15, 51, 52, 53, 64, 67, 68, 69, 73, 79, 84, 102, 103, 114, 134, 140
career, 3, 14, 32, 54, 96, 102, 103, 104, 105, 107, 131, 135
celebrate, 96, 100, 115, 116, 133, 141
challenges, xvii, 1, 4, 66, 71, 77, 79, 82, 83, 90, 96, 117, 137

Subject/Name Index

changes, xi, 1, 3, 12, 13, 14, 24, 31, 32, 34, 58, 69, 71, 75, 84, 117, 118, 137, 140
Chapman, G., 31, 110, 150
childrearing, 3, 21, 23, 32, 102, 103, 135
children, 7, 12, 13, 15, 16, 20, 23, 25, 30, 35, 40, 49, 66, 81, 96, 97, 102, 103, 104, 105, 136, 143
China, 20, 36
choosing to love. See love
Christian, xvii, 17, 26, 30, 44, 45, 86
circumstances, 24, 80, 88, 106, 121, 128
civilization, xiii, 6, 11, 12, 14, 16, 25, 26, 138
climax, 94, 95
cognitive, xi, 3, 4, 41, 42, 115, 124, 134, 138, 139, 140
cognitive level, xviii, 50, 113, 123
cognitive restructuring, xviii, 143
collective unconscious, 21, 27, 141, 143
college, 104
Collins, G. R., 29, 150
commitment, xiii, xix, 2, 3, 27, 28, 31, 32, 33, 35, 36, 42, 43, 45, 46, 47, 48, 49, 50, 51, 53, 78, 82, 83, 84, 85, 89, 92, 96, 99, 103, 105, 107, 109, 110, 111, 112, 114, 115, 116, 117, 120, 124, 128, 132, 133, 139, 140, 144, 145, 147
communal family. See family, types of
communication, 2, 29, 30, 32, 33, 35, 50, 72, 91, 103, 112, 113, 115, 117, 118, 119, 120, 123, 132, 133
  definition of, 118, 143
  effective, 33, 72, 113, 117, 118, 120, 123
  paradoxical, 120
  process of, 97, 121, 122, 123, 124
  levels of, 118, 119, 123
  marital, 115, 121, 123, 145
  skills of, 41, 113
  styles of, 120
  ways of, 119
companionship, 102, 109
compassion, xvii, xviii, 4, 43, 44, 45, 46, 47, 48, 49, 50, 51, 53, 74, 77, 83, 99, 110, 128, 133, 134, 137, 138, 139, 140, 141, 145
  definition of, 44, 143
complementation, 143
compliments, 97, 133
compromise, 44, 81, 133
conceptualization, xi, xvii, 18, 43, 46, 78, 93, 121, 137, 140
concluding, 123, 145
condition, 19, 26, 75, 85
conflict, 2, 33, 35, 52, 79, 82, 104, 117, 124, 125, 126, 132
  definition of, 143
  development of, 35, 104, 124, 125
  in marriage, 31, 126
  management of, 33, 35, 70, 124
  marital, 32, 35 143
  resolution skills, 120
confusion of feelings, 83
conjugal, 23, 24
connecting, 80, 122, 145
consanguineous family. See family, types of
consequences, 28, 90, 117
conservative, xiii, xiv
cope, 30, 97
co-provider, 103
costs and benefits. See attraction
counseling, xviii, 76, 92, 96, 103, 107, 109
  premarital counseling, 98
courtship, 20
Covey, S. R., 1, 3, 11, 30, 87, 89, 106, 150
Creator, 9, 22, 63, 64
credit, 55, 97
cultural, xiii, xiv, xv, xvi, xvii, 1, 2, 3, 14, 20, 30, 36, 38, 60, 113, 137, 138, 140, 145, 146
culture, 1, 3, 12, 17, 19, 25, 36, 38, 86, 101, 146

D

dating, 17, 20, 91, 95
Davidson, B. S., xi, xix, 12, 72, 98, 151, 156

debts, 136
decision, 3, 9, 35, 42, 49, 52, 78, 81, 82, 83, 94, 123, 134, 143, 144
  head, 81,
  heart, 81, 82
  marital, 21
  personal, 52
  rational, 81
  willful, 52
dependency, 43, 147
desire, 26, 30, 41, 44, 48, 49, 52, 56, 58, 59, 60, 78, 84, 94, 110, 139
detoxification, 100
development, 5, 11, 20, 25, 37, 88, 89, 102, 103, 107, 122, 124, 125, 133, 134, 139, 144
differences, 17, 29, 31, 33, 38, 61, 64, 81, 82, 129
disengagement, 113
dividends, 107, 120
divorce, xv, xvii, 1, 2, 23, 25, 27, 32, 34, 36, 48, 64, 68, 103, 134, 137
dreams, 89, 96
dual-career, 3, 14, 24, 144, 155
Dunlap, K., 3, 12, 13, 14, 15, 18, 19, 20, 23, 24, 25, 26, 151
dysfunctional, 33, 74, 143

E

economic, xiii, xiv, xvii, 2, 3, 13, 14, 24, 31, 115, 144
education, xviii, 13, 14, 36, 54, 55, 76, 104, 106, 135, 144
egalitarian, 2, 3, 4, 8, 35, 88, 103, 141
  ideal, xvi, 87, 139, 140, 141
  marital relationship, 138
  marriage, 3, 4, 19, 22, 63, 102, 109, 134, 135
  paradigm, 27
  philosophy, xvii, 85, 88
  principle, 134
  relationship, 32, 85, 101, 103, 110, 133, 138, 139, 144
egalitarianism, xi, xv, xviii, 2, 3, 4, 24, 25, 27, 69, 84, 85, 86, 87, 88, 89, 99, 101, 103, 105, 107, 108, 109, 111, 113, 115, 138, 140, 141
  definition of, 144
Ellis, H., 2, 18, 26, 27, 55, 144, 151
emergency, 90, 91
emotion(s), 2, 25, 44, 45, 59, 81, 82, 84, 111, 113, 115, 119, 120, 122, 124, 125, 126, 132, 139, 144, 147
emotional needs, 13, 43, 49, 99, 109, 110, 138
empowerment, 2, 48, 53, 89, 105, 144
  definition of, 144
  in marriage, 2
enemy, 115, 120
engagement, 34, 107, 114, 139
engaging, 93, 98, 122, 124, 145
Engels, F., xiii, 5, 6, 7, 16, 23, 151
enmeshment, 64
equality, vii, xvii, 5, 6, 7, 8, 9, 10, 14, 18, 24, 27, 32, 63, 64, 65, 66, 72, 87, 102, 144, 145, 147
experiences, 2, 11, 12, 22, 42, 49, 68, 80, 81, 91, 93, 98, 102, 131, 132, 133, 141
evolution, 7, 11, 12, 14, 32
  evolutionary, xvii, xviii, 6, 16, 17, 18
exogamy, 17, 144
expression, xix, 33, 44, 52, 74, 84, 95, 112, 128, 138
external, 29, 48, 56, 119, 143

F

fail, 32, 34, 36, 83, 88, 117, 137
failings, 96
family, xi, xiii, xiv, xv, xvi, xvii, 1, 3, 5, 6, 7, 8, 9, 11, 12, 13, 14, 15, 16, 18, 19, 21, 25, 27, 32, 33, 34, 35, 65, 96, 98, 101, 102, 103, 104, 115, 117, 120, 129, 130, 134, 144
  commitment, 109
  definition of, 13, 14, 144
  finances, 134, 136
  financial security, 135
  functions of, 12, 13
  income, 104, 134

family - continued
    level of, 128
    life cycle, 78, 102
    patriarchal, xiv
    relationships, xi
    systems, 12, 18
    types of, xiii, 6, 12, 15, 322, 10, 143, 145
feeling, 43, 50, 52, 53, 67, 72, 75, 75, 87, 94, 97, 99, 111, 113, 114, 122, 124, 126, 140
level, 122
Feldman, R. S., 35, 36, 37, 38, 39, 41, 42, 48, 97, 115, 151
female, 6, 8, 9, 15, 17, 19, 22, 23, 30, 54, 56, 57, 59, 62, 65, 94, 95, 98, 101, 132, 137, 140, 144, 145, 146
    chastity, 23
    inferiority, 1, 25,
    fidelity, 16
    liberation, xvii
    sexual response, 56, 57, 59, 94
    subjugation, xiii, 10, 85, 86
    virginity, 23
femininity, 10, 101
feminism
    gender, xiv, xv
    liberal, xiv, xv
    radicalized, xiv
finance, 32, 91, 134, 135, 136. See also family, finances
forgiveness, xvii, xviii, 3, 4, 44, 45, 49, 50, 83, 99, 112, 126, 133, 139, 139, 143
    definition of, 144
    levels of, 99
free, 23, 62, 71, 72
    choice of marriage, 20, 21,
    sexual intercourse, 7
friendship, 39, 41, 42, 91, 130
frustration, 92, 97
    marital, 115
fulfillment, 72, 73, 100, 110, 116
    personal, 36, 110
    need, 43, 73, 130, 147
    sexual, 109

G

garden. See marriage, metaphors of
gender, xiv, xv, 2, 8, 30, 32, 38, 61, 139, 146
generation, xvii, 1, 2, 27, 103
gifts, 95, 110
giving, xi, 16, 17, 30, 43, 48, 56, 68, 87, 91, 93, 98, 103, 115, 116, 117, 118, 119, 133, 136
God, 8, 9, 22, 45, 51, 53, 63, 115, 147
golden rule. See marriage, golden rule of
Gray, J., 31, 109, 152
group marriage. See marriage, types of
grow, 71, 75, 108, 116, 130, 131

H

Haralambos and Holborn, 12, 13, 14, 23, 24, 40, 103
Harley, W. F., 31, 73, 94, 109, 152
heart, 49, 50, 51, 52, 72, 81, 82, 95, 99, 100, 101, 108, 110, 113, 114, 123, 124, 123
    compassionate, 110
    hardened, 77, 100
    hardening of, 95, 99
    of compassion, 83
    servant, 87
Hebrew, 44, 45
hierarchy, 9, 41
Hindu, 20, 44
historical, xiii, xiv, xv, xvi, 5, 6, 11, 15, 18, 44, 45, 55, 58
historicity, vii, xv, xvii, 11, 54, 93, 95, 138
hope, 24, 97, 100, 106, 114, 123, 145
human brokenness and bondage, 44, 45, 46, 49, 50, 51, 77, 83, 99, 115, 138
human history, 4, 6, 8, 11, 12, 26, 137
human physiology, 95
humor, 41, 96, 133
hypothesis, 17, 40

I

identification, 64, 105
imagineering, 106, 145
implementation, 105, 138
independence, xvii, 3, 24, 41, 103, 136, 147
individualism, xvii, 137, 138, 140,
Industrial Revolution, xiii
inferior, 2, 19, 20, 25, 26, 64, 96, 97, 140, 145, 146
inspection, 69, 105
intentionality, 75, 84, 90, 100, 145
interaction, 33, 34, 37, 39, 40, 43, 66, 131
interdependence, 3, 43, 136, 146
internalize, 40, 68, 74, 89
intimacy, xviii, 4, 25, 33, 34, 42, 43, 46, 47, 48, 49, 50, 51, 53, 59, 66, 82, 83, 97, 102, 105, 108, 115, 116, 128, 129, 130, 131, 132, 139, 140, 144, 145
introspection, 44, 100, 143
Islamic, 18, 19, 44

J

Jesus, 22, 147
Jewett, P. K., 63, 64, 65, 153
Jewish, 16, 17, 22
job, 36, 78, 104, 107, 131
Judeo-Christian, xvi, xvii, xviii, 16, 17, 45, 63, 145
Jung, 21

K

kindness, xix, 114
kingdom, 52
Knowledge, 45, 55, 56, 75, 76, 92, 103, 131, 143

L

laughter, 96
leadership, 4, 101, 138

Lewis Henry Morgan. See Morgan
life, xi, xviii, 1, 8, 13, 25, 26, 27, 44, 48, 49, 50, 65, 66, 67, 70, 71, 78, 80, 84, 85, 89, 92, 95, 96, 97, 98, 102, 105, 106, 108, 113, 114, 116, 117, 130, 131, 132, 134, 135, 137, 139, 141, 144, 145, 146
Lifelong, 80, 107, 111, 115
liking, 37, 39, 41, 42, 80, 81, 146
listening, 113, 120, 126
literature, xi, xv, xvii, 2, 3, 4, 6, 19, 29, 31, 44, 45, 57, 59, 130, 134, 137, 140
loner, 97
looking glass self, 40, 145, 147
love, xvii, 2, 3, 4, 13, 20, 28, 29, 33, 35, 36, 37, 38, 41, 43, 44, 45, 46, 47, 48, 49, 50, 51, 52, 53, 54, 64, 66, 68, 74, 75, 77, 78, 81, 82, 83, 84, 86, 87, 89, 90, 91, 93, 95, 96, 97, 98, 99, 109, 110, 112, 114, 116, 127, 128, 132, 133, 140, 144, 145, 147
    accommodative, 49, 50
    aimless, 47, 48, 49
    as pulley-wheel, 52
    associative, 50
    authentic, 4, 46, 51, 52, 53, 74, 77, 79, 81, 83, 84, 99, 127, 128, 129
    bank, 21
    components of, 42, 46, 51, 99, 145
    cycle, 77, 78, 79, 84
    Johari window of, 46, 47, 145
    language, 31, 110
    letter, 93, 95, 112, 113
    life, 48
    maps, 29
    marital, 74, 77, 78, 79, 128, 139, 140
    maker, 92
    marriages, 20
    relationship, 39, 42, 48, 49
    self-giving, 85
    triangle, 42
    types of, 42, 46, 59, 83, 145
love making, 93, 132
    cycle of, 93, 144
love triangle. See love

M

MacKinnon, C., xv, 153
magnet. See marriage, metaphors of
male, xv, 8, 9, 15, 17, 22, 23, 24, 30, 56,
   61, 65, 94, 95, 98, 101, 132, 137,
   140, 143, 144, 145, 146
  biased, 23
  dominance, xiii, xvi, 1, 6, 10, 23, 25,
   27
  sexual response, 56
man, 7, 8, 9, 11, 18, 19, 22, 23, 26, 27, 38,
   40, 47, 48, 51, 55, 61, 63, 64, 83,
   91, 109, 146
  as male and female, 22
marathon. See marriage, metaphors of
marital, vii, ix, xiv, xv, xvii, 3, 19, 24, 25,
   28, 30, 31, 32, 33, 34, 45, 66, 68,
   69, 69, 72, 73, 74, 75, 77, 78, 79,
   81, 83, 91, 93, 107, 115, 116, 128,
   131, 134, 137, 138, 139, 140, 146
  atmosphere, 35
  automaticity, 75, 76
  commitment, 27, 28, 36
  communication. See
     communication, marital
  conflict, 32, 35
  cycle, 33
  decision(s), 20, 21
  dissatisfaction, 29, 30
  failure(s), xvi, xvii, 28, 33, 34, 35, 36,
     117, 137, 139, 140
  frustration, 115
  functions, 13
  happiness, 2, 31, 61, 138
  identity, 65, 66
  inequality, 19, 23
  intimacy, 128, 130
  issues, xi, 31, 100, 134
  journey, 2, 84
  preparation, 98
  problems, 2, 4, 21, 28, 29, 30, 31, 74,
     115, 139
  reflection, 115
  relationship(s), xi, xiii, xv, xvi, xviii,
     1, 3, 4, 29, 30, 32, 33, 61, 66, 69,
     78, 92, 97, 102, 108, 109, 117,
     120, 130, 131, 132, 133, 134, 135,
     138, 139, 140, 141
  satisfaction, xvii, 2, 28, 29, 30, 34,
     45, 60, 76, 87, 117, 128, 129, 130,
     134, 135
  seasons, 105
  skills, 4, 52, 75, 78, 117
  stability, 31, 103, 134, 135
  success, 2, 4, 31, 34, 35, 66, 99, 137,
     138, 139
  systems, 18, 19
  tension, xv
  unhappiness, 28
  union, xvii, 4, 67, 116, 137
marriage, xi, xii, xiii, xiv, xv, xvi, xvii,
   xviii, 1, 2, 3, 4, 5, 7, 8, 9, 12, 13,
   14, 15, 16, 18, 19, 20, 21, 22, 23,
   24, 26, 27, 28, 29, 30, 31, 32, 34,
   35, 36, 46, 49, 52, 53, 55, 60, 63,
   64, 65, 66, 67, 68, 69, 70, 71, 72,
   73, 75, 76, 77, 80, 81, 82, 87, 89,
   90, 91, 92, 95, 97, 98, 100, 101,
   102, 103, 104, 107, 109, 111, 115,
   117, 120, 127, 128, 131, 132, 133,
   135, 137, 138, 139, 140, 141, 143,
   144, 146
  aim of, 64
  art and science of, 108
  commitment, 36
  conceptualization of, xi, 137, 140
  conflict in, 31
  critical periods in, 103
  definition of, xiii, 6, 145
  egalitarian, 3, 4, 19, 22, 63, 102, 109,
     134, 135
  failure, 34
  forms of, 6, 7, 18, 21, 24
  function of, 25
  golden rule of, 73, 74, 141, 147
  healthy, 3, 97, 100
  historicity of, 138
  inequality in, 24
  institution of, 98, 138
  intimacy in, 130
  investment in, 107
  master plan of, 77, 78
  metaphors of, 69, 70, 72, 140, 146

money in, 134
patriarchal, 17
permanence of, 22, 71
purpose-drive, 75
rates, 32
relationship(s), xi, 25, 32, 36, 63, 124, 138, 140
resilient, 139
roles in, 101
servanthood in, 85, 91, 92
sexual relation in, 92
sexuality in, 140
stages of, 102
successful, 3, 4, 20, 25, 29, 31, 108, 137
system of, 17
tasks of, 104
trial, 2, 147
types of, 15, 16, 18
Marxian Socialism, xii
masculinity, 101
Masters and Johnson, 56, 57, 58, 59, 62, 154
matching phenomenon, 38, 145
mate, 20, 22, 38, 104, 111
matriarchy. See family, types of
matrifocal. See family, types of
maturity, 31
memories, 81
men, xi, xvi, 2, 4, 8, 9, 10, 15, 18, 19, 20, 21, 23, 24, 25, 31, 32, 38, 50, 58, 60, 61, 65, 72, 92, 101, 104, 109, 128, 129, 130, 134, 143, 144, 145, 147
metaphor, 69, 109. See also marriage, metaphors of
mindset, xi, xvi, xvii, 3, 27, 69, 83, 138, 141
model of love, 99
money, 3, 24, 29, 30, 31, 97, 133, 134, 135, 136
monogamy. See marriage, types of
moral, xiv, 28, 44, 50, 53, 88, 89
Morgan, 5, 6, 11, 14, 16, 153, 154
motivation, 41, 58, 133
motor vehicle. See marriage, metaphors of

movement, xiv, 24
  physical, 94
  women's, xiv, xv, 14, 27
Murdock. See Peter Murdock
mutual submission, 86, 87
Myers, D., 21, 28, 35, 36, 37, 38, 39, 40, 41, 42, 43, 48, 51, 52, 80, 83, 96, 97, 120, 130, 145, 154

N

need fulfillment, 43, 73, 130, 147
needs, 13, 23, 29, 30, 31, 33, 36, 42, 43, 49, 73, 75, 84, 90, 91, 92, 96, 99, 101, 105, 109, 110, 138, 139
Neiger, S., 55, 56, 57, 61, 154
Nichols, M. P., 117, 119, 120, 154
Nisbet, J. F., 18, 19, 20, 26, 27, 154
non-normative influences, 102, 104
non-verbal behaviors, 112
normative influence, 102, 104
norms, 14, 18, 20

O

opportunity, xvii, 1, 67, 106, 116
orgasm, 56, 57, 58, 61, 62, 94

P

paradigm, xvii, xviii, 3, 4, 25, 27, 67, 68, 69, 74, 75, 81, 94, 107, 111, 114, 136. See also paradigm shift
paradigm shift, 3, 10, 27, 86, 138, 146
paradoxical communication. See communication, paradoxical
parenting, 103
parents, 12, 15, 20, 40, 103, 105, 131
passion, 20, 40, 42, 43, 46, 47, 48, 49, 50, 51, 53, 82, 83, 87, 116, 128, 132, 139, 140, 145
patriarchal, xi, xiii, xiv, xv, xvi, xvii, 2, 3, 4, 5, 8, 9, 10, 14, 17, 18, 19, 21, 22, 23, 25, 27, 31, 32, 60, 63, 68, 69, 85, 86, 88, 101, 103, 138, 139, 140, 141

patriarchal family. See family, patriarchal
patriarchy, xvi, xvii, xviii, 4, 9, 15, 17, 18, 23, 27, 31, 86, 101, 137, 138, 140, 141, 146
patrifocal. See family, types of
penis, 62, 93, 94
perfect, 6, 7, 46, 52, 53, 82, 96
perfection, 83
permissive, 133
personal, 1, 15, 20, 23, 28, 35, 36, 37, 39, 43, 52, 91, 98, 107, 110, 135, 136, 143, 144, 145
personality, 29, 31, 33, 34, 43, 63, 66, 71, 72, 147
perspective, xi, xvii, 3, 6, 9, 12, 14, 16, 17, 21, 22, 24, 33, 44, 55, 71, 72, 74, 94, 102, 103, 104, 115, 125, 134, 137, 141
Peter Murdock, 12, 13
phenomenon, 2, 5, 7, 13, 21, 37, 38, 40, 41, 43, 109, 137, 140, 144, 145
pheromones, 39, 40
philosophical, xiii, xiv, xv, xvi, 44, 46, 134, 137, 140, 141
physical attractiveness, 37, 38, 80, 146
physical intimacy, 34, 130
playful, 96
polyandry. See marriage, types of
polygyny. See marriage, types of
positive, 4, 13, 34, 35, 37, 40, 41, 44, 45, 48, 50, 71, 83, 85, 89, 109, 113, 115, 128, 129, 135, 144
possibility, 1, 24, 30, 98, 104
potential, xv, 2, 3, 18, 20, 23, 38, 50, 71, 77, 100, 114, 128, 133, 134, 141, 144
power struggle, 3, 29, 32, 35, 102
premarital counseling. See counseling, premarital
presupposition(s), 5, 6, 8, 9, 16, 146
priority, 74, 85, 89, 97, 135
proactive, xv, 4, 87
problem solving skills, 120
process(es), xv, xix, 2, 4, 20, 21, 23, 28, 40, 50, 58, 59, 66, 67, 70, 82, 92, 93, 97, 98, 99, 100, 102, 106, 118, 119, 120, 121, 122, 123, 124, 126, 131, 132, 143, 144, 145, 146, 147
processing, 119, 123, 126, 145
product thinking. See thinking
promiscuity, 5, 6, 7, 8, 14, 16, 17
property, xiii, xiv, 7, 8, 15, 16, 17, 23
prospecting, 123, 145
provider, 7, 103
provider-servant role, 86
proximity, 37, 39, 71, 80, 81, 146
psychological, xv, xvi, 13, 20, 25, 30, 32, 34, 42, 52, 55, 59, 64, 65, 66, 71, 93, 95, 102, 104, 115, 118, 130, 135, 139
psychology, xviii, 2, 21, 67
punaluan family. See family, types of
purpose-driven marriage. See marriage, purpose-drive

Q

qualification(s), 9, 104
question(s), 1, 2, 5, 9, 55, 106, 108, 109, 110, 112, 122
   situation related, 108
   situational, 112

R

rationalization, 125
reactive, 33, 87
reason(s), xvi, xvii, 11, 14, 21, 22, 27, 28, 31, 36, 38, 39, 51, 58, 78, 80, 94, 106, 114, 135, 140
recipe(s), 2, 90, 99
reciprocity, 51, 73, 74, 84, 110, 138, 141
   of liking effect, 39, 146
   within the self, 141
relationship(s), xvii, 1, 2, 3, 4, 7, 9, 21, 25, 28, 29, 30, 31, 33, 34, 35, 37, 38, 39, 40, 41, 42, 43, 44, 45, 46, 47, 48, 49, 50, 52, 59, 60, 64, 65, 66, 68, 69, 75, 76, 77, 80, 82, 83, 84, 88, 90, 92, 95, 96, 97, 98, 99, 100, 101, 105, 107, 108, 110, 111, 112, 114, 115, 117, 120, 124, 125, 128,

130, 131, 132, 133, 134, 135, 138, 139, 146, 147
atmosphere in, 45
automaticity in, 100
channel of, 117
commitment in, 36, 45
communication in, 112
compassion in, 48, 99
conflict in, 52
dating, 95
dual career, 24, 102, 144
egalitarian, 4, 32, 85, 101, 103, 110, 133, 138, 139, 144
family. See family relationships
feelings in, 105
growing edge of, 99
healing power of, 97
healthy, 48, 68, 82, 111, 124
interpersonal, 38, 43, 106, 120
intimate, 2, 28, 35, 43, 45, 82, 83, 100, 120
intimacy in, 50, 129, 132
lifelong, 115
longevity of, 45
long-standing, 82
love, 39, 48, 49, 84
male-Female, xi, xv, xvi, xviii, 3, 8, 85, 87
marital. See marital, relationship
marriage. See marriage, relationship
patriarchal, 18
polygamous, 19
promiscuous, 14
romantic, 2
satisfying, 3
sexual, 9, 13, 16, 108, 128
successful, 33
religion, 17, 21, 25, 26, 29, 30, 81
remarriage, 2, 103, 137
reproduction, 13, 144
resilient, 71. See also marriage, resilient
re-socialization, xviii, 146
responsibility, 3, 13, 21, 27, 35, 48, 68, 107, 109, 140
   childrearing, 23, 103
   domestic, 24
   individual, 100, 144

man's, 64
personal, 45
social, 28
Robert Sternberg, 42, 46
role(s), xi, xv, 8, 9, 29, 100, 101, 103
   conjugal, 23, 24
   co-provider, 103
   gender, 32
   gender-based, 8
   leadership, 101, 138
   sex-roles, 3, 31, 101
   sexual, 8
   social, 3, 14
   spousal, 33
romance, 43, 59, 132, 147

S

sacrifice(s), 69, 87, 91
Santrock, J. W., 21, 25, 29, 31, 33, 37, 38, 42, 97, 155
satisfying, xi, 3, 23, 92, 94, 136
savagery, 6, 11, 12, 14, 14, 15, 16, 23, 138
seesaw. See marriage, metaphors of
self-disclosure. See communication, levels of
self-giving love, 85
self-revelation, 43, 147
servant, xvi, 85, 91
servanthood, xvi, 85, 86, 87, 89, 91, 92, 95
service, 69, 87, 88, 89, 90, 91
   a recipe for daily, 90
   acts of, 110
   community, 105
   joy in, 89
   quadrants, 88
   security in, 89
   unconditional, 85
sexual, 13, 14, 16, 21, 23, 24, 26, 30, 56, 57, 58, 92, 94, 115, 129, 144
   ability, 56
   activity, 56
   adjustment, 4
   anxiety, 61
   appetite, 92

sexual - continued
    arousal, 58, 59
    attachment, 16
    behavior, 17, 18, 54, 55, 56, 58, 133
    cohabitation, 14
    desire, 26, 41, 59, 92
    disorders, 59
    dysfunction(s), 30, 31
    frequency of intercourse, 61, 60
    fulfillment, 109
    function, 13, 56
    identity, 30
    intercourse, 7, 26, 30, 59, 61, 64, 94
    interest, 30, 56, 59
    intimacy, 108, 131, 144
    histories, 55
    life, 66
    morality, 14
    need(s), 13, 23, 92
    neutrality, 59
    permissiveness, 55
    phases of, 56
    positions for, 61, 62
    problems, 58
    prowess, 92
    relationship. See relationship, sexual
    relation(s), 14, 23, 92, 144
    release, 59, 94
    research, 54
    response(s), 54, 56, 57, 58, 59, 60
    response cycle, 56, 58, 59, 94
    revolution, 14
    roles, 8
    satisfaction, 4, 60, 61, 92, 128
    tension, 57, 58
    union, 2
sexuality, xvii, 4, 21, 26, 30, 31, 54, 56, 58, 59, 93, 94, 95, 140, 147
similarity, 31, 34, 37, 38, 55, 66, 81, 82
sin, 9, 26
slavery, xiv, 23, 85
society, xiii, xvi, 12, 19, 23, 31, 34, 40, 144
    capitalist, xv
    contemporary, xv
    patriarchal, 23
    Western, 14
socio-cultural, xiii, xvi, 1, 2, 3, 27, 59, 68, 137, 139, 140
socio-economic, xi, 8
special occasions, 97
spiritual equality, 8, 147
spouse, 30, 48, 52, 53, 66, 67, 68, 69, 71, 72, 73, 74, 75, 89, 90, 92, 95, 96, 97, 109, 110, 111, 112, 113, 114, 115, 121, 122, 123, 124, 126, 128, 130, 133, 134, 139, 140
steps, xi, 70, 75, 99, 141
Sternberg. See Robert Sternberg
stimulate, 4, 20, 95, 113, 131
submissive, 9
successful marriage. See marriage, successful
successive approximations, 141
sum thinking. See thinking
swimming, 70, 108

T

Talmey, B. S., 11, 14, 19, 61, 62, 155
teamwork. See marriage, metaphors of
tension, xv, 6, 10, 35, 57, 58, 99, 112, 126
tests, 82, 83
theological, xvi, xvii, 5, 6, 8, 14, 25, 27, 85, 86, 87, 138
theology, xv, 3, 27, 85, 139
theory, 6, 15, 38, 40, 43, 65, 147
thinking, xiv, 3, 25, 65, 68, 73, 74, 81, 89, 109, 113, 121, 132, 135, 136
    critical, xix
    level of, xviii, 1
    patriarchal, 85
    proactive, xv
    product, xi, xv, xvi, xvii, xviii, 3, 4, 64, 65, 67, 68, 69, 73, 77, 84, 85, 87, 88, 89, 90, 94, 99, 100, 102, 107, 108, 109, 110, 114, 125, 127, 128, 132, 134, 135, 137, 138, 139, 140
    sum, 64, 67, 73, 89, 109, 137, 138, 139, 140, 146
    way of, 1, 3, 27, 68, 140, 147

thought, xi, xiii, xv, xvi, xix, 1, 3, 8, 42, 47, 50, 59, 85, 91, 108, 137, 138, 143
time, 1, 8, 12, 19, 21, 39, 41, 50, 56, 67, 68, 70, 71, 73, 74, 75, 76, 80, 90, 92, 93, 94, 95, 96, 97, 98, 102, 104, 105, 106, 107, 108, 110, 111, 112, 113, 114, 122, 125, 130, 131, 132
trial marriage. See marriage, trial
trial(s), 2, 82, 83, 92, 107
truth, 41, 69, 74, 100, 114
Turner, J. F., 43, 152

U

unconditional, 44, 85, 89
union, xviii, 2, 3, 4, 42, 47, 48, 49, 63, 64, 65, 66, 67, 68, 98, 115, 116, 141
unmet needs, 36
unresolved feelings, 97
unresolved issues, 34, 91, 97, 98

V

vagina, 57, 58, 62, 93
values, xiv, xv, 19, 29, 33, 35, 47, 59, 81, 87, 146, 147
virginity, 23, 24
vision, 75, 87

W

water. See marriage, metaphors of
weaknesses, 45, 51, 72, 74, 82, 87, 98, 115
Westermarck, E. A., 5, 7, 16, 156
western. See society, western
wheel theory of love, 43, 147
willfulness, 52
willingness, 3, 30, 41, 52, 58, 59, 77, 82, 92, 109, 124, 127, 143
women, xi, xv, xvi, 1, 2, 3, 4, 6, 8, 9, 10, 14, 15, 17, 18, 19, 20, 21, 23, 24, 25, 26, 27, 31, 32, 38, 40, 57, 58, 59, 60, 65, 72, 103, 104, 109, 128, 129, 134, 143, 144, 145, 146, 147
   as chattel, xiv
   chastity of, 23
   in ministry, 3
   independence of, 24
   liberation of, xvii, 14, 27
   mobility of, 104
   needs of, 109
   oppression of, 23, 31
   repression of, 1
   role(s) of, 23, 27, 101
   struggle of 10
   suppression of, 10
   treatment of, 17, 21, 23
   veiling of, 25
work, 21, 24, 27, 33, 96, 103
writing, 70, 95, 133

Y

young, 32
   couples, 92
   marriages, 32
   people, 2

www.ingramcontent.com/pod-product-compliance
Lightning Source LLC
Chambersburg PA
CBHW051931160426
43198CB00012B/2109